RAISE THE STANDARD
a practical handbook for raising ethnic minority and bilingual pupils' achievement
based on successful policy and practice in cities across the European Community

compiled by Phil Green for DIECEC

Trentham Books

First published in 1999 by Trentham Books Limited

Reprinted 2000

Trentham Books Limited
Westview House
734 London Road
Oakhill
Stoke on Trent
Staffordshire
England ST4 5NP

© DIECEC 1999, 2000

British Cataloguing in Publication Data
A catalogue record for this book is available from the
British Library
ISBN 1 85856 127 2

Designed and typeset by Trentham Print Design Ltd., Chester and printed in Great Britain by Cromwell Press Ltd., Wiltshire.

Contents

Foreword

Bart Bambury, *Chef de File*, DIECEC Network, 1996-1998

By far the most valuable and cherished memories and experiences of my life as an educator relate to activities where I worked in collaboaration with colleagues on behalf of children or young people on an educational initiative or project. On such occasions, my isolation as a teacher or teacher educator was forgotten. My colleagues' vision, dedication, expertise and willingness to learn helped uplift and enthuse me. The end product, whether a teaching approach or learning materials, was always better than I could have achieved on my own. Shared experiences, values and commitment bestowed added depth and value to the undertaking. The children or young people, as prime beneficiaries of the work, certainly gained value from our endeavours. I, as a teacher and learner involved in the creation of new work, was also un-doubtedly changed and re-energised.

This publication is the result of collaborative, transnational sharing and endeavour. It represents the combined efforts of a wide range of people from European cities who share a common goal – to improve the educational opportunities, quality of life and life chances of children and young people who are excluded, marginalised or otherwise disadvantaged, especially those from ethnic minority backgrounds. The issues and challenges posed to schools and education systems by the increasing numbers of such learners in schools across the European Union and more widely have neither gone away nor been satisfactorily addressed. The gap between their achievement levels and those of their peers has, in general, widened rather than reduced. The DIECEC cities present this Handbook as a synthesis of policy and practice which has made a positive difference, in the hope that its messages will prove useful to all those who can have an impact on children's and young people's development.

I continue to be amazed by the extent to which people from different European cities, from a wide range of educational contexts, cultural and linguistic backgrounds, can work together to produce innovative, practical and successful responses to these challenges. In the end, we have all recognised that we have more in common than we thought, that our linguistic and cultural differences are small compared with our common goals and aspirations and that our processes of working together are more important than the specific contexts in which we work. Colleagues have agreed to recognise, value and share experiences, initiatives and projects in a spirit of endeavouring to address the challenges which face us and, above all, excluded and marginalised children, young people and their families.

On behalf of the DIECEC Network, I would like to thank DGXXII of the European Commission for its support for the network's activities. Particular thanks are also due to the many people within the DIECEC cities who have contributed to this publication, and to Phil Green the network co-ordinator and compiler of this Handbook.

Bart Bambury, City of Cork Education Centre, November, 1998

SECTION ONE
THE OVERALL PICTURE

Introduction to this DIECEC
state of the art Handbook

This Handbook has been produced by the DIECEC cities, through their city representatives and many different people working within their education systems, including teachers, headteachers, other staff in schools, educational advisers and inspectors, staff in education departments and other departments of city, regional and provincial administrations. There is more about DIECEC overleaf.

From 1994-1998, DIECEC developed, implemented and evaluated transnational education projects, each involving a number of the DIECEC cities and their schools, to seek to develop policy and practical actions which will improve the quality of education provided for children and young people from ethnic minority backgrounds and enable them to achieve at considerably higher levels. In addition each city has developed policies, practice and projects which have the same aims.

The issues discussed in the Handbook are both difficult and contentious. DIECEC offers this publication as an overview and synthesis of actions which have proved or are proving to be successful. The Network has always wished to discuss and debate the issues, but more importantly to develop and engage with policy and actions which really make a difference. We do not expect that everyone reading the Handbook will agree with all it says. However, we do have an increasing body of evidence that the basic approach – multi-level developments which scaffold children's education and development at home and in their community as well as through a good school – works. In that sense, we believe that it is time for a focus on what makes a difference, rather than a more debate of the issues. It is in this spirit, and with a sense of humility, that the Handbook has been compiled.

The DIECEC Network is about to become a non-profit-making European Association. It owes its existence and continuing development to the member cities, the dedication and perseverance of the city representatives and especially of the Steering Committee, the support of a wide number of other organisations including DGXXII of the European Commission, whose financial assistance has made this publication possible, and the work undertaken 'on the ground' by schools, youth services, community groups and other public, private and voluntary bodies, with children and young people. They are our future, and the future of Europe and the world. Investing in them in a very significant, coherent and co-ordinated way in the initial, formative years of their education and personal development (we mean up to at least the age of 20!) has to be a major priority for every member state of the European Union. We hope that this Handbook will contribute to ensuring that this significant level of financial and human investment is made in ways which have a positive impact.

The Development of DIECEC

DIECEC (Developing Intercultural Education through Co-operation between European Cities) is a transnational network and non profit-making Association of European cities working together to improve the intercultural education of all pupils and to raise the achievement levels of pupils from ethnic minority backgrounds.

As this Handbook goes to press, the member cities of the DIECEC Network are:

Athens	Antwerp	
Birmingham	Bologna	Bradford
Cork	Greenwich (London)	Helsinki
Linkoping	Madrid	Marseille
Motala	Odense	Oslo
Rotterdam	Sheffield	Turin
Udine	Vienna	

It is envisaged that DIECEC will continue to expand to embrace cities in the new member states of the European Union and other cities from member states already in the network.

The Network is co-financed by the European Commission, mainly through the COMENIUS Chapter of the SOCRATES Programme administered by DGXXII – Education, Training and Youth. DIECEC's main focus is on improving the achievement levels of ethnic minority pupils, but much of its work is relevant to the broader group of educationally disadvantaged pupils in cities, suburban and rural areas.

Multi-Level Working – a fundamental principle

The basic principle of DIECEC's approach to intercultural education and raising the achievement levels of pupils from ethnic minority backgrounds is 'multi-level working'. This is defined in more detail in Section 3. Briefly, it means that every project will affect several of these different levels:

- individual pupils
- groups of pupils
- parents/guardians
- teachers
- other school staff
- other professionals
- schools
- neighbourhoods or communities
- the city and/or whole education system

The multi-level approach inevitably embraces the concept of multi-agency or multi-disciplinary working, the co-ordination, where appropriate, of a wide range of public, private and voluntary sector organisations, services and people who can support the education and learning of children and young people and parents or guardians in their role as prime educators of their children.

Multi-level working takes full account of the learning of children and young people in school, at home and in their community or neighbourhood. One challenge of multi-level working is to bring the three vertices of this triangle into harmony so that there is effective support, or scaffolding, for learning in all three contexts.

DIECEC has accumulated strong evidence that ways of working according to this multi-level approach are highly effective in improving the achievement levels of ethnic minority pupils, and can enhance the quality of life of their families. Schools play a key role but this Handbook shows that the best results are achieved when other agencies actively contribute, and it offers practical guidance to policy makers and practitioners who have a responsibility towards ethnic minority children and young people on implementing these approaches. The multi-level approach can benefit all educationally disadvantaged pupils.

A brief chronology of the Network

The Eurocities Social Welfare Committee held discussions in 1994 about the difficulties children and young people from ethnic minorities encounter in their education. Four cities – Birmingham, Marseilles, Rotterdam and Turin – began reciprocal study visits, co-financed by DGXXII, to exchange ideas and examples of good practice in meeting the challenges posed by increasing numbers of ethnic minority children and young people in their cities. So began DIECEC.

By 1997, the now enlarged Network decided that it was time to share their work and made a bid for funding for a 'state of the art' handbook, a practical guide to intercultural education and raising achievement through the multi-level approach. This is the result.

The DIECEC Network has always been a network of cities operating for the benefit of ethnic minority pupils, their families and communities. It has also always been a network of people who come to know each other well, have confidence in each other's strengths and expertise but are also always open to representatives of new member cities.

In 1998, the first steps were taken towards Europe-wide Thematic Networks on raising achievement and intercultural education, involving a wide range of other European projects and networks. DIECEC will play a key role and the Network website and newsletter will continue to communicate and disseminate ongoing practice.

DIECEC is run and administered by the cities themselves. The DIECEC cities have important things to say to other cities in Europe, as this Handbook shows. None of the cities individually, nor indeed the Network as an entity, would claim to have all the answers to the challenges of raising achievement and developing intercultural education for all pupils. Therefore DIECEC plans to develop and expand its work, to work closely with others, and to add to the synthesis of knowledge, understanding and successful work begun in this Handbook.

How to use this handbook

T he Handbook has not been designed to be read from page 1 through to the end. Rather, its sections have been written so that they can be more or less self-standing, so long as the reader has some understanding of the basis of DIECEC's work.

So we recommend that you start by reading sections 1–5, which cover the background, set the context, explain some key principles and generally set the scene. After that, you may find it best to go to the sections or themes which interest you most. For example, if you work in a school, you may want to see Section 9 as a priority, followed by some Themes from Section 10 which are particular issues for you; if you are interested in the role of cities and those responsible for education systems, then Section 8 would be a suitable starting point, maybe followed by Section 9.

If your main interest is in a particular theme (for example, engaging parents as the prime educators of their children), then select that theme, with its accompanying case studies, within Section 10. This might then lead you back to Sections 9 and 8 and broader considerations about how schools and education systems can develop their policies and approaches.

The Handbook, then, is intended as a work of reference rather than a 'one-off' read. We hope you will want to dip into it again and again, looking at different sections. Above all, we would want you to end up by consistently asking yourself this question 'How, in my role, can I help to ensure effective multi-level solutions to the issues which affect the achievement levels of ethnic minority children and young people?' Such solutions will impact on the learners themselves, parents, teachers, the whole school, the local community, leisure time and (in the best examples) the whole education system. They will also involve true partnerships with many people and organisations.

We hope that you will also come to agree that intercultural education itself is a major factor in raising achievement; that helping to ensure that children and young people are ready to learn, feel comfortable with themselves and other people, know that they are valued as individuals whatever their background and know that they can achieve, is as vital to helping them achieve at high levels as their knowledge about subjects in the curriculum.

If you find yourself thinking and acting in ways which help to bring this about, whatever your involvement in children's and young people's learning, then the Handbook will be serving its purpose. We wish you success and fulfilment in these endeavours.

Key Words used in this Handbook

Achievement: by achievement, DIECEC means not just success in recognised quali-fications and the attainment of good grades or marks against national benchmarks or expectations. These are crucial, but so is achievement in terms of personal, social, spiritual, moral and cultural development. Achievement in areas such as the arts, sport, community service and caring for others also comes within this broad definition, as does the concept of citizenship and the skills required to play a positive and active role as a member of a society or community. The development of employment-related skills and attitudes is also key. DIECEC promotes opportunities for the development of the 'whole person'. Central to the achievement levels of children and young people from ethnic minority backgrounds is their self-esteem or self-image. DIECEC believes that the recognition of achievement in areas which have not always been recognised and valued at home or at school is important in terms of its enhancement of self-esteem.

City: The cities in DIECEC vary in their responsibility for educational services. 'City' is used as a broad term to indicate all the organisations which have a statutory or formal responsibility for some or all of the education system and the provision available to the people who live there. In this Handbook, 'city' means 'all those organisations with a responsibility for education and related-services which operate within the city as a geographical entity', including the specific responsibilities and services provided by a city as the Local Authority.

Where, as in Southern Europe, responsibility for education is assumed by the Province or Region, and the name of the city is synonymous with the Province and/or the Region, 'city' means all three organisations and implies co-operation between them. This same applies to any other city, on the grounds that, in the multi-level approach, no single body has responsibility for all the services, organisations and people which affect the educa-tion and learning of children and young people.

DIECEC sees the 'city', in the sense of the organisation or organisations with respon-sibility for the quality of life of its citizens (often, but not always, the 'Local Authority'), as the organisation which must take the lead in developing the multi-level approach at the level of the whole education and learning system which operates within it.

COMENIUS: part of the SOCRATES programme of the European Commission. It co-funds school education-related projects, including projects in the area of intercultural education. See also 'DGXXII' and 'SOCRATES' below.

Community: this word is used in two senses in the Handbook: firstly, to denote the community or ethnic or other group to which people belong. DIECEC understands that it is not sufficient to speak, for example, of 'the Moroccan Community' as though it were one homogenous group, but it usefully designates the main community. The second sense of 'community' is the total local community.

DGXXII of the European Commission: DGXXII is currently one of 24 Directorates-General of the European Commission. DGXXII is concerned with the development and implementation of policy and practice at European level in the areas of Education, Training and Youth. The COMENIUS programme is one sub-section of the SOCRATES programme concerning education in schools and is currently partly targeted on the development of intercultural education.

Ethnic Minority: this phrase is something of a compromise and, after much debate, it is used to denote the children, young people and families whose ethnic background differs from the dominant ethnic background of the city in which they live – not just people who have a different skin colour from the majority community, but any minority community which is in danger of exclusion, underachievement, marginalisation and alienation and whose educational needs are different or additional partly as a result of their heritage and of faith, cultural and linguistic differences with the majority community.

Intercultural Education: this means learning to value and respect people from different cultural backgrounds, so also their culture, language, faith and traditions. Unlike multicultural education it implies active appreciation of different cultures and developing skills which enable people from different backgrounds to interrelate. So it is an important feature of the education of all children, young people and adults, a means of combating racism and xenophobia and of preparing people for life in an increasingly pluralistic society. DIECEC's approach is to emphasise also the commonality and similarities of apparently different cultures, faiths and traditions, and the richness of diversity.

Mother Tongue: the first language learned by children and the language they mostly use at home in early childhood. DIECEC understands that children may speak several languages at home so 'home language' can be confusing. Where children learn two or more languages equally from a very early stage, they could be considered to have two or more mother tongues. DIECEC distinguishes between 'mother tongue' and 'second or additional language' on the grounds that a clear understanding is necessary of the processes of acquisition of these languages and the interrelationship of the processes of learning them.

Scaffolding: scaffolding is used in the construction of a building to support it and enable its construction. As the building is finished, the scaffolding or parts of it can be removed and the building will be self-sustaining. Further scaffolding may be needed if the building is to be extended or repaired. DIECEC uses the word as an analogy the support structure of education at school, in the home and in the community required for ethnic minority pupils to achieve well. Elements of this support structure are also 'scaffolding', for example, providing additional opportunities for children to extend their command of their second language.

Second Language: this term is used to denote what is a second or additional language to be learned because it is the main, or one of the main, languages of everyday communication in the country. DIECEC accepts and understands some of the arguments in favour of using the term 'additional language', but has chosen not to use it by itself on the grounds that it does not distinguish the all-important context in which the language is being learned – in other words is does not separate the notions of learning foreign languages from second or additional language learning. In places in the text, the phase 'second or additional language' is used to reinforce DIECEC's view that this can mean the same thing.

Transnational Working: transnational is used in the sense of working across and between cities in different national contexts. It implies genuine collaboration between the member cities of the Network. DIECEC knows from experience that transnational working is essential to developing solutions which draw on different experiences and ideas from different cities to produce better solutions for different contexts.

Key aims, challenges and principles

The two cental aims of the DIECEC Network are

- to develop and improve the intercultural education of all children and young people so that they acquire:

  - a positive view of diversity

  - the knowledge, skills and understanding to value different cultural, faith and linguistic backgrounds

- to raise the achievement levels of children from ethnic minority backgrounds from birth upwards, in the context of the broad definition of achievement set out above.

Removing the stigma of underachievement

Underachievement can have a devastating effect. Children can leave school without possessing the basic tools for further learning and future success. Underachievement affects individual choice, quality of life, economic and social inclusion or exclusion and, perhaps most critically, self-esteem. Far too many young people (across the DIECEC cities, between 10 and 20%) fail to complete statutory schooling with any recognised qualification or with negligible accredited success – or drop out altogether. Among them are a disproportionately large number of young people from ethnic minority backgrounds and this is true also of pupils formally or informally excluded from schools and those designated as having special educational needs. Although a few may eventually achieve some level of success through tenacity, hard work and good fortune, the overwhelming majority are condemned by their underachievement to be always at the end of the queue. Their own lack of success is often reflected in the poor achievement of their children. DIECEC's work is about breaking this cycle of underachievement.

This stigma of underachievement is not inevitable, nor is it acceptable. It is a key principle of DIECEC that combating underachievement must continue so that more young people achieve fulfill their potential. No city or country can afford underachievement. The people it affects are, in effect, thrown on the scrap-heap. Whilst local, national and European initiatives (second chance schools, welfare to work, access programmes) may rescue some young people, these normally treat only the symptoms and not the root causes of underachievement. Primarily curative measures such as second chance schools are valuable but the great majority of DIECEC's activity is designed to prevent failure and underachievement occurring in the first place.

In many instances, children are at risk of failure from birth not because they lack intelligence but because their early and continuing development is not well scaffolded.

The Challenges

DIECEC regards the growing ethnic diversity in European cities as enriching to the cultural, faith, linguistic and social character of the cities and of Europe. At the same time, this welcome feature of all European cities presents a number of challenges to schools and city councils, regional and provincial organisations and other bodies and services with formal responsibility for education systems.

The word 'welcome' reflects the official attitude and policy of the DIECEC cities towards ethnic minorities but this does not necessarily mean that all cities have a universally positive approach to cultural, faith and linguistic diversity. There is evidence that racist attitudes, negative and stereotypical views and xenophobia still prevail at all levels of society and across a broad range of organisations. Intercultural education represents a considerable and fundamental challenge to cities but fits their concerns for social harmony and cohesion, and for the economic prosperity and quality of life of their citizens.

Racism and xenophobia present major problems for cities. So do the educational levels attained by children and young people from ethnic minority backgrounds. DIECEC is not seeking to blame schools, parents, the pupils themselves, cities, or national governments and systems, but to develop, discover, analyse, evaluate and disseminate effective interventions which consistently make a positive difference.

What really makes a difference to learning?
The common factor across Europe

It is ultimately the interactions of children and young people in their capacity as learners with skilled teachers, tutors and other adults – including parents – which make the difference; improving the quality, quantity and frequency of these interactions has to be the final goal of schools, city and education system leaders, and also of heads of other relevant public services, leaders and managers of private and voluntary organisations and anyone else who is or should be concerned with education in a community and the consequences for social and economic well-being. DIECEC's evidence is that if these positive interactions are confined to one context, or if they do not occur in more than one of the three contexts of home, school and community, then ethnic minority and other children will often underachieve, no matter how effective the school's internal processes.

Quality, quantity and frequency of interactions between learners and teachers

All the different structures, administrative and financial arrangements and ways of working in different cities, education systems and member states all result in the same basic situation: day in, day out across the European Union, in over 320,000 schools and other centres of learning, children and young people interact with teachers, support teachers, tutors and other people who can help them to learn; it is indeed the quality, quantity and frequency of these interactions which make the difference.

Responding to, engaging and empowering communities

The history of interventions designed to help young people and families of ethnic minority origin is littered with examples of worthy and often valuable work which has, essentially, been done to them rather than with them and this has often created a dependency culture. A good number of communities are now demanding that their own definitions of need be addressed and that they be involved in the planning, implementation and evaluation of all ameliorating initiatives. DIECEC welcomes these moves as a vital step towards communities becoming self-sustaining socially, economically and educationally.

It is a principle of DIECEC's work that local communities and especially ethnic minority communities should actively participate in decisions about improving the situation for them and their children, and be fully involved as providers and learners in educational opportunities for themselves and their children inside and outside school. This assists the process of empowering communities to take appropriate responsibility for areas of their children's learning as a part of the work of schools.

As DIECEC knows from its wide experience of working in favour of ethnic minority pupils, some specific additional resources are required to scaffold their education if they are to have good opportunities to learn in the contexts of home, school and community. Many of the cities provide additional resources, for example to reduce class sizes in the early years of education, to provide additional teaching in second language and mother tongue, and to provide pre-school education. DIECEC takes the view that these additional resources are essential and that they will be needed for a considerable time; many young residents of the second and third generation will enter formal education with little or no command of the language of their city. The principles of early intervention set out below certainly apply here – the earlier and more effective the scaffolding, the lower the cost in terms of additional resources in the longer term. Cities and education systems must respond to the irrefutable research evidence that children's second or additional language learning needs to be scaffolded for between five and seven years – and this requires additional resources.

Other resources which are not within the control of the city, school, or other body with formal responsibility for the education system can contribute greatly to the multi-level approach. They are human, financial and material and are in the hands of other public, private and voluntary sector services and organisations. Many of them are already used to provide additional educational and recreational opportunities, but they are rarely linked to the aim of raising achievement levels or co-ordinated with mainstream educational funding. A principle of multi-level working is that these resources too must be co-ordinated at city and school level in order to implement multi-level working, which does not rely so much on additional resources as on the co-ordination of what is already available.

Partnership working

Multi-level working implies partnership between all the services, organisations and, above all, people who can help children and young people to learn. In DIECEC's experience, partnership is easy to speak about but difficult to implement in the true spirit of recognising the equal or appropriate value of the contribution of other people to the effective scaffolding of children's and young people's education.

Take for example the roles of parents or guardians as the prime educators of their children. How parents and guardians fulfill these roles is crucial to the achievement levels of their children. Cities, schools and other organisations can merely fulfill statutory requirements towards them but essentially keep them at bay. They can be open and welcoming to them as a school but ignore their actual or potential role as educators. It is a consistent feature of successful multi-level schools in DIECEC cities that they regard parents as the prime educators of their children, see them as vital to their success and work with them on as equal a footing as possible so that they can support their children appropriately.

Another feature of this different approach to parents is to see them as bringing skills, experiences, knowledge and understanding (of their children, but also of life!) which can contribute to the education provided by or through the school. Ideal models of consultation with parents regard teacher, child and parent as equal partners when discussing and evaluating progress and agreeing targets for which each of the three parties contract to assume specific responsibilities.

This approach with parents is one example of a way of thinking and acting which is essential to a successful multi-level approach. All who can contribute should work together towards a multi-level approach and with a clear understanding of and respect for their differing roles – including the children and young people themselves.

The principle of early intervention

DIECEC takes the view that providing an effective support system or scaffolding for children's education can never start too early. Work in the cities shows that intervention with parents even before children are born, pays dividends. Positive early childhood development is demonstrated by research to lead to higher achievement and fewer difficulties later on. The nature of these early learning experiences is a matter of considerable debate, both within the DIECEC cities and across the member states. The evidence suggests that education systems which delay the introduction of formal learning until the age of six outperform those which place more emphasis on these aspects from the age of four, and that there are wider and long-lasting social benefits of this policy.

Early intervention demands a multi-level approach because a wide range of agencies and services is involved with the families concerned. This requires a co-ordination of work, recognition of roles and responsibilities and a clear focus on enabling parents to help their children develop in ways which will support their future education. Responding to the absolute priority of early intervention may well require a redirection of resources.

Multi-level scaffolding of children's and young people's education

The essential features of approaches which raise the achievement levels of ethnic minority children and young people are proven and they are underpinning principles of DIECEC's approach. They are:

- an approach which recognises that effective education involves learning at home, at school and in the community

- harmony and co-operation between these three potential contexts for learning

- consistent scaffolding of learning from a very early age to the point where the young people can operate as independent learners and achieve levels of success which match their potential

- policy and practice which consistently address the three contexts – home, school and community – and which operate at a number of different levels, including those of the children or young people, the school, parents or guardians, the community and the city or whole education system.

The reasons for putting multi-level scaffolding in place

DIECEC has come to the very clear conclusion that the multi-level approach is effective because:

- analysis of successful practice in the cities reveals that children's education is well scaffolded in the three contexts of home, school and community

- many schools condsidered good or effective and where pupils do well can rely on existing scaffolding or are working hard with receptive parents and others to put it in place

- even in well-regarded schools, there can be significant numbers of ethnic minority pupils who underachieve because no scaffolding is in place outside school or because the school is not in harmony with their home and community; this underachievement may not show up in published statistics or reports

- where the multi-level approach is implemented elsewhere, for example in certain American cities, research also indicates that a multi-level approach makes a measurable difference

- the policies and practices developed within the DIECEC cities and their schools indicate that significant improvements occur where an effective multi-level multi-agency approach operates.

Recognising, evaluating and disseminating good practice

DIECEC quickly found that despite considerable differences in the contexts in which they work, all the cities had existing examples of good practice which could be a source of learning for others. Some could identify the mistakes they had made and projects which had failed, and why they had gone wrong, so helping others to avoid the same pitfalls.

These learning experiences are not confined to transnational working; all the cities have arrangements for ethnic minority pupils which they take for granted (because they have been in place for a long time) which are in fact new ideas for others. The cities have begun to recognise that much of what they already do is valid and valued, and the cities have learned from each other. Recognising, disseminating and celebrating good practice are thus key elements of DIECEC's operation.

The DIECEC cities

This section contains brief context information designed to help readers to understand something of the context in which the DIECEC cities are working. You may wish to refer to these statements when considering particular case studies, as well as the specific context information provided within each of the case studies.

There is no doubt that the particular situation in each city can make a significant difference to the nature and extent of provision for pupils. For example:

- the basis on which statutory and non-statutory education are provided

- the responsibilities of different authorities and services for the education system

- the extent to which schools are able to make their own decisions within a national, regional or more local framework

- ways in which teachers and additional financial and human resources are deployed

The context information is not there to explain how certain things can be done or why they cannot. Whilst the context makes a difference, it does not prevent the challenges from being addressed. Certainly the organisations responsible for different parts of the education system can make it more or less easy to tackle problems by their degree of flexibility and the extent to which they collaborate with others. If some of the most complex situations can bring about successful multi-level solutions – as they do in many of the DIECEC cities – there is no reason why other, similarly complex arrangements cannot be made to put similar provisions in place. In the end, the willingness, ability and capacity to do this depend more on human than on administrative or structural factors. At this level, strong political and professional leadership become crucial factors at city and education system levels; at school level, headteachers can be a potent force for change and development.

So we ask our readers to consider the contexts of the cities, but not to see them as determining the capability or capacity of the DIECEC members to bring about improvements.

Antwerp

City population: 448.354

Percentage of population of ethnic minority origin: 59.389%

School population: 62.466 (450 schools: public, Catholic and a few special schools)

Percentage of school population of ethnic minority origin: 12.333 %

Highest percentage of ethnic minority pupils in any one school: 100%

Number of schools with additional resources to meet the needs of ethnic-minority pupils: 76

Main ethnic minority groups: Moroccans – Turks (non EU citizens)

Main community languages: Arabic (Berber), Turkish

Athens

Population: 3,450,400

School Population: 329,700

Percentage of school population of ethnic minority origin: 5%

Highest percentage of ethnic minority pupils in any one school: 60%

Number of schools with additional resources to meet the needs of ethnic-minority pupils: 145

Main ethnic minority groups: Albanians, Russians, Philippinos, Egyptians, Kurds

Main community languages: Greek

Bologna

Population: 404,400

Percentage of population of ethnic minority origin: 4.5%

School population for which the city is responsible: 25,194

Percentage of school population of ethnic minority origin: 5%

Highest percentage of ethnic minority pupils in any one school: 20%

Number of schools with additional resources to meet the needs of ethnic minority pupils: 15

Main ethnic minority groups: Moroccan, Philippino, Former Yugoslavian, Albanian, Chinese, Bangladeshi, Sri-Lankan, Ethiopian, Pakistani

Main Community Languages: Arabic, Serbo-Croat, Albanian, Cantonese, Bengali, Tamil, Urdu/Panjabi

Birmingham

Population: 1,016,700

Percentage of population of ethnic minority origin: 22%

School population: 176,500

Percentage of school population of ethnic minority origin: 40%

Highest percentage of ethnic minority pupils in any one school: 100%

Number of schools with additional resources to meet the needs of ethnic minority pupils: 230

Main ethnic minority groups: Pakistani, Indian, African Caribbean and Bangladeshi

Main Community Languages: English, Urdu, Panjabi (Urdu), Panjabi (Gumurkhi), Bengali, Gujarati

Bradford

Population: 485,000

Percentage of population of ethnic minority origin: 20%

School population: 86,800

Percentage of school population of ethnic minority origin: 31%

Highest percentage of ethnic minority pupils in any one school: 100%

Number of schools with additional resources to meet the needs of ethnic-minority pupils: 112

Main ethnic minority groups: Pakistani, Hindu, Bangladeshi, African-Caribbean

Main Community Languages: Panjabi-Urdu, Panjabi-Gumurkhi, Gujerati, Bengali

Cork

Population: 164,000

School population: 30,000

Percentage of school population of traveller or ethnic minority origin: 5%

Highest percentage of traveller or ethnic minority pupils in any one school: 10%

Number of schools with additional resources to meet the needs of traveller and ethnic minority pupils: 12

Main ethnic minority groups: Travellers, Chinese, Pakistani, African-Caribbean

Main Community Languages: Panjabi-Urdu, Panjabi-Gumurkhi, Gujerati, Bengali, Cantonese.

Helsinki

Population: 539,000

Percentage of population of ethnic minority origin: 4,5%

School population: 88,300

Percentage of school population of ethnic minority origin: 7%

Highest percentage of ethnic minority pupils in any one school: 18%

Number of schools with additional resources to meet the needs of ethnic minority pupils: almost all of the school providing for ethnic minority pupils

Main ethnic minority groups: Russian, Estonian, Somalian

Main Community Languages: Russian, Somalian

Linkoping

Population: 132900

Percentage of population of ethnic minority origin: 4.7%

School population: 13,825

Percentage of school population of ethnic minority origin: 7%

Highest percentage of ethnic minority pupils in any one school: 20%

Number of schools with additional resources to meet the needs of ethnic minority pupils: all schools

Main ethnic minority groups: Bosnian/Herzegovinian, Iranian, Scandinavian

Main Community Languages: Serbo-Croat, Arabic, Kurdish

Madrid

Population: 5,022,300 (region), 2,867,000 (city)

Percentage of *Population of Ethnic Minority Origin*: 1.89% or 100,000 people. Illegal immigration is estimated at 30,000 people above this figure.

School population: 900,000

Percentage of school population of ethnic minority origin: 2.5%

Highest percentage of ethnic minority pupils in any one school: 15%

Main ethnic minority groups: European (Portuguese, former Yugoslavia etc.), North American, Central American and Caribbean, South American, Asian, African, Oceanian.

Odense

Population: 189.000

Percentage of population of ethnic minority origin: 7%

School population: 16.399

Percentage of school population of ethnic minority origin: not available

Highest percentage of ethnic minority pupils in any one school: 76,6%

Number of schools with additional resources to meet the needs of ethnic minority pupils: Out of 35 schools in Odense only 5 do not receive additional resources, but considering the number of ethnic minority pupils, 6 schools receive substantial additional resources

Main ethnic minority groups: Turkish, African(a large community of Somalis), Vietnamese, Iranian and Iraqi

Main Community Languages: the languages of the groups indicated above

Oslo

Population: 510,000

Percentage of population of ethnic minority origin: 10,8%

School population: 57,100

Percentage of school population of ethnic minority origin: 27.8%

Highest percentage of ethnic minority pupils in any one school: 91%

Number of schools with additional resources to meet the needs of ethnic minority pupils: practically all schools

Main ethnic minority group: Pakistani

Main Community Languages: Panjabi-Urdu, Arabic, Turkish, Somali, English, Vietnamese, Spanish, Tamil, Albanian

Rotterdam

Population: 590,000

Percentage of population of ethnic minority origin: 41%

School population: 144,000

Percentage of school population of ethnic minority origin: 52%

Highest percentage of ethnic minority pupils in any one school: 100%

Number of schools with additional resources to meet the needs of ethnic minority pupils: 180

Main ethnic minority groups: Surinamese, Turks, Moroccans, Southern Europeans

Main Community Languages: Turkish, Arabic, Portuguese

Sheffield

Population: 530,000

Percentage of population of ethnic minority origin: 6.98%

School population: 70,068

Percentage of school population of ethnic minority origin: 12.13%

Highest percentage of ethnic minority pupils in any one school: 95%

Number of schools with additional resources to meet the needs of ethnic minority pupils: 43

Main ethnic minority groups: Pakistani, Caribbean, Yemeni, Somali, Bangladeshi, Chinese

Main Community Languages: Panjabi, Urdu, Arabic, Bengali, Somali

Turin

Population: 910,000

Percentage of population of ethnic minority origin: 3.03% (27,620) – this figure refers to people who are registered as residents – there are several thousands of non-registered people, and the number of newcomers is increasing

School population: 68,000 (3-14 year-olds)

Percentage of school population of ethnic minority origin:

age 3-5 : 6%
age 6-10: 4%
age 11-14: 3%
age 15-18: 1%

Highest percentage of ethnic minority pupils in one school: 45%

Number of schools with additional resources to meet the needs of ethnic minority pupils: 20

Main ethnic minority groups: Moroccan, Peruvian, Chinese, Philippino, Romanian, Egyptian, Somalian, former Yugoslavian, Nigerian, Senegalese, Albanian

Main Community Languages: Arabic, Spanish, Cantonese, Serbo-Croat, Albanian

Key components of developing multi-level working

Leadership

Throughout this Handbook the principles of community involvement and consultation, and of 'bottom-up' developments are stressed. Vital also is strong, effective political and professional leadership and commitment – not in a controlling or autocratic sense but a high profile commitment to the goals and processes inherent in the multi-level approach, and the leadership and managerial skills to work through difficult and complex processes to change attitudes, policy and practice.

The object is to find those who can undertake this leadership role with the people involved and empower them. And who can forge the necessary partnerships of parents, professionals and others in the public, private and voluntary sectors. Effective multi-level approaches need their champions and their strong advocates at every level. DIECEC believes that the following components are all essential to a sound process for developing multi-level working:

Audit, analysis and evaluation

Assess your current provision critically against the criteria indicated in Section Two (if you work within a city or organisation with responsibility for the education system) or Section Three if you work in a school. You may want to assess your current arrangements against the criteria and policy measures in other sections of the Handbook as well, for example against some or all of the Themes explored.

Ask: Why do pupils in one school do so much better than those in another similar school? Why does one ethnic minority group perform much better on average than another? Why do ethnic minority pupils attain highly in one subject area but not in another in the same school?

Using such data, identify the major issues under headings like: 'basic skills', 'literacy', 'attendance', 'achievement levels at age 11', 'achievement of boys compared with girls' etc. You may believe that you can identify these issues without using the data, but this has been part of the problem – people assuming that they know what the issues are without acquiring any objective evidence.

It is vital that this data is available for analysis according to ethnicity and background. Your city or school must have reliable baseline data about children and be able to measure and chart their progress, otherwise you cannot address your effectiveness nor identify children and young people at risk of failure soon enough.

Identifying relative strengths and weaknesses

Analyse the audit and identify strengths, weaknesses, overlaps and gaps in current provision for ethnic minority children and young people, in line with the factors set out in this Handbook.

Prioritise tackling the weaknesses and gaps in relation to what is known as a result of your audit. Look at the strengths and see what you can learn from them. **Will this Handbook help you to formulate some ideas about those areas which are most likely to have a major effect?**

Engage with local communities and service providers

If no suitable arrangements for genuine community consultation exist, this too should be made a priority. Be willing to draw on the skills, knowledge and understanding of parents and other members of the community in the identification of priorities and planning and managing developments.

Identify a small number of priorities for action

Identify and agree with the communities maybe two or three issues for immediate attention and for developing a multi-level, whole community approach. For example, if improving literacy is a priority, treat this as a whole community issue and determine the role and contribution of the communities themselves, schools, parents, providers of adult and continuing education, local voluntary bodies and relevant national or regional agencies. Approach other priorities in the same way and assign other issues to later years, but have a schedule for tackling them.

Identify a few indicators of success and agree some targets

For each priority, agree with those involved a small number of hard-edged, measurable indicators which will be used to establish the baseline and measure progress. For example, in the area of basic skills: the percentage of pupils reading below expected levels at the age of 7 or 8; the percentage of pupils achieving levels above the expectation, differentiated according to ethnicity and background. Three or four clear indicators are better than 20 vague and unmeasureable ones.

For each priority, agree for each indicator a realistic but challenging target within agreed timescales. If the target is longer term (for example, a reduction of 80 percentage points over three years in the number of children reading below expected levels), agree 'milestone targets' for each year of the plan (say, 20% in year one, 25% in year two, 35% in year three).

Plan of action

Draw up an action plan. Make sure you include the performance indicators already agreed, and plan carefully how the evaluation will at every stage be built in to the baseline sketched out in your audit. Plan in detail for year one and leave the rest of the plan more flexible.

Whichever priorities you chose, the Handbook is likely to offer relevant guidance. Look at the examples of practice and consider how you could use or adapt them to your own needs. All have proved effective.

Implement the Plan

Follow the action plan and keep it on track. Make sure those responsible for implementing parts of it are aware of the exact nature of their contribution and the deadlines. Hold regular but short and tightly-managed meetings to review action and modify it when necessary.

Communicate the process and outcomes of your plan

Many initiatives founder because they are not well communicated. Take every opportunity to communicate. Use existing systems wherever possible, including newsletters, committee reports, the media, word of mouth and presentations, especially with the communities involved. Show people that it is working and do not be too modest! Boast a bit about the successes and give credit to the people who deserve it. Make your team, and the community, feel good about themselves, and talk up the success. This helps build a culture of achievement. If you take this part of the process seriously, the value of involving the communities will soon be apparent.

What progress have you made?

Take time out for a breather, and to assess where you have got to and discuss where to go from here. The questions which follow can be used for personal reflection and also for a 'team' review meeting of all those involved in this multi-level project:

- What did you learn about the data you have available to analyse and audit the current position? Is it good enough? What do you need to do make it fully reliable?

- What have you learned about consulting with the community and incorporating their ideas? Is this basic requirement of multi-level working working to the full?

- Have you been able to hand over the management of any priority issues to the community or individuals within it? The community will not become self-sustaining unless you do so. Has the community managed any of the work from the start?

- What have you learned about the process of identifying and working on priorities? Did you try to do too much? Could you have taken on more? (a rare event!)

- What have you learned about multi-level working and the development of effective partnerships? **Compare what you have done with some of the relevant examples of good practice in the Handbook**. Ask yourself who else should have been involved in the work, and how you could now involve them.

- What do you know about the outcomes of the work so far? What progress has been made? Has children's reading improved, and how do you know? Are they attending school more regularly? Are more parents coming to consultation evenings? Can more parents support their children's work effectively at home? How many children are attending homework clubs? How many new activities are there out of school time? How many children are attending them? In each case, ask the hard questions not the easy ones, and focus on the hard-edged performance indicators.

- Where do you go from here? What else needs to be done? Your answers to the questions above should be informing your action plan for the next sixth months or year.

We expect that people will argue with these components and with the processes suggested. They are offered as a way of identifying priorities, planning, implementing and reviewing effective actions. But what is important is to have a process which covers the essential components and, above all, engages and empowers the communities concerned. You may wish to make this your starting point.

Evaluation: a multi-level approach

Working at different levels means evaluating processes and outcomes at some or all of the following levels: the individual pupil, groups of pupils, teachers, parents, schools, neighbourhoods and at city or education system levels. In each case, the process of evaluation, including the instruments used and the evidence collected, has to be fit for determining level, working processes and outcomes.

Valid and relevant evaluation is essential to any development or change process, to identify the starting point or baseline, where and to what extent things must or could change, and to assess the extent to which change is effective. Good baseline information is essential to multi-level approaches, indeed to any approach.

At each level it is important to know the answers to basic questions. At the level of pupils:

- how are individuals and groups of pupils (for example, children from different backgrounds, boys and girls) currently performing in basic skills?

- how much progress do they make in a given timespan (for example, one school year)?

- how are different groups performing overall, for example, ethnic minority pupils compared with the overall school population?

- do the same pupils perform differently in different classes or subjects?

At teacher level:

- what is the current baseline for the quality of teaching in each class, year group or department?

- how are the needs of ethnic minority pupils reflected in curriculum planning?

- do expectations of ethnic minority pupils match the expectations of other children in the school and nationally?

- to what extent do teachers feel they have the additional knowledge, skills and understanding to work successfully with ethnic minority pupils?

At city, education system and schools levels:

- what data is available about young children to schools when children enter them? What information is available from other services (social, welfare etc.)? Do nursery and primary schools have sufficient information about their new pupils?

- how do outcomes for pupils compare across the city, and with other similar cities?

- how does the performance of pupils in different schools with a similar 'profile' of pupils compare?

- to what extent are parents engaged with their children's education?

- how are the skills and knowledge of parents recognised and valued as an important contribution to their children's education?

- to what extent are school open to their communities?

- what information is there at city level to help schools and the education system identify priorities? Where should the city target scarce additional resources?

- how do the results produced by one system (for example in one area of a member state) compare with those of comparable children in another? If there are differences, then what is making the difference?

1.1 *The uses of data and information to chart progress, inform planning for change and set targets*

Baseline information is essential but of limited value by itself, even when it corresponds to the different levels DIECEC is targeting. Without reliable, on-going evaluation, using relevant indicators and valid assessment methods, neither the effects of change nor progress from the baseline can be identified. It is important to ensure that a reliable and valid process is in place to chart progress, both in terms of processes which are known to be important to learning (for example, the quality of teaching in a school) and of outcomes (for example, pupils' levels of competence in basic skills, and their attendance at school).

Simply charting pupils' progress will not by itself change anything. Analyses of data and reliable qualitative assessments must be used to identify issues and problems (for example, a weakness across a large number of schools in reading or in number skills, specific problems relating to the performance of girls in science, the attendance levels of pupils from a particular community) and to inform actions or interventions. Data can help schools and education systems decide, for example, whether a problem in performance in mathematics is related to a generally low level of performance in the subject, or to a particular area (for example, the concepts of shape and space), or to cultural differences or linguistic difficulties. Only then can actions be planned.

Decisions about priorities for action may be taken on the basis of what appears easiest to address, or of whim and influence. Planning for action with local communities, as suggested in Section 6, will be a much better-informed process if reliable data is available.

Well thought-out action to address an identified need based on an analysis of reliable information is essential for school improvement, and must include realistic but challenging targets. A challenging but achievable percentage increase on the current baseline is a suitable target. It will seek to accelerate progress or move significantly to close the gap on comparable schools – but it will not be a figure plucked out of the air or an 'educated guess'. It will relate specifically to an aggregation of the current achievement levels of the target group of pupils.

1.2 *The relevance of data to the achievement levels of ethnic minority pupils*

There are good examples across the DIECEC cities of data being used to identify baselines and issues, inform actions, set targets and assess progress – mostly in countries where data is readily available about school performance of individual pupils at different stages. The professional use of rigorous, valid and reliable evaluation is essential to raise achievement, especially for ethnic minority children, whose underachievement may be masked by a generally satisfactory picture. This data must exist, or be developed, at a number of stages in the school system, otherwise action required will be identified too late for the pupils who need it. Experience suggests that objective data about individual pupils' progress in basic skills should be collected, analysed and acted upon annually.

In schools where ethnic minority pupils represent a low percentage of the pupil population – especially where this percentage is not statistically significant – their needs and performance can be hidden and overlooked when reporting at school level. Similarly, in schools with a very high percentage of pupils from ethnic minorities, whether in a multicultural, bicultural or almost monocultural pupil population, expectations and targets may tend to reflect a stereotyped view of their achievement potential.

Consequently, schools need to be able to compare their performance and operation with the highest achieving schools nationally with a similar pupil profile, and with the highest achieving schools overall. National education systems as well as cities and other local bodies with responsibility for the education system need to provide schools with comparative data which enables them to identify the levels at which their pupils could or should be performing, and what they should do to bridge the gap. An approach of this kind justifies the uses of raw data. Using the data simply to make unfair comparisons between schools with vastly different contexts is distinctly unhelpful to the process of improvement.

Any comparison should also look beneath the surface of schools which perform at very different levels with similar populations. Does the high achieving school have effective scaffolding for learning in the contexts of home, school and community? If so, the school providing good education but achieving lower outcomes for its pupils needs to be able to identify this as a factor to address, instead of just working harder and harder for minimal improvements. Or has a high achieving school in an area of high ethnic minority settlement found effective ways of reflecting the culture of its pupils in its curriculum and trained its staff on this issue? External inspection reports on schools do not always identify these factors as contributing to high achievement, because they are not currently recognised as vital to the process of raising achievement by those who establish the inspection and evaluation criteria.

Schools and education systems should expect the degree of improvement for ethnic minority pupils to be no lower than for others; in fact, given the level of support which many pupils from ethnic minority backgrounds receive from their extended family, there is good reason to set more demanding targets. The evidence for this is available – a substantial and increasing number of schools in the DIECEC cities can demonstrate that emergent bilingual pupils entering school with little or no command of the main language of the city at the age of four achieve at the national expectation by the age of seven.

2. Elements of evaluation

2.1 *Pupils and groups of pupils*
Various schemes for assessing children at the start of school are used in DIECEC cities. Schools need good baseline data about their pupils when they enter the school on

- language competence

- practical skills and competences

- social skills

- information about home languages, faith and other relevant elements of their background

Every school, whatever its age range, should also collect, analyse and use on an on-going and regular basis information about pupils' attainment levels in:

- basic skills, both mother tongue and second or additional language, particularly measures of the four language skills (including reading with understanding, not just reading mechanically)

- mathematics, with an emphasis on addition, subtraction, multiplication and division

- information and communications technology skills

Affective elements are important to learning but they are more difficult to measure. Self-esteem, attitude to school and to education, other measures relating to social and emotional development can be significant to learning and progress, especially for ethnic minority children. Whilst not wishing to overstate the case, DIECEC believes that for ethnic minority pupils, self-esteem and the question of identity are especially important.

Schools should undertake regular soundings of pupils' opinions of the school and their education and act accordingly. These areas can be assessed by a combination of observations and questionnaires, but information can also be gained through class and school councils and by simply talking with the pupils.

The data collected should also include attendance, parental support, homework, participation in extended educational activities and peer relationships. Evidence shows that peer relationships and the dominant ethos within peer groups can hugely affect achievement. For example, where the dominant ethos in a class or year group is not to take schoolwork seriously, or to do the minimum possible to get by, schools need to identify this quickly and do something about it – with parents and others.

Although schools and education systems need to be mindful of data protection issues, it is vital that individual pupil data – anonymised where necessary – including indicators of ethnic and other origin and of gender, is used at other levels: class, school, neighbourhood and city, for example. Without this data, one DIECEC city would not have been able to identify that its schools had a problem over poor basic skills in mathematics with pupils from some ethnic minority backgrounds – and to deal with it with increasing success.

Pupil level data is essential for schools to develop overviews of pupil outcomes at class, year group and whole school levels. Through these processes, schools can achieve a snapshot at any time but, more importantly, also a view of development over the years of individuals and cohorts of pupils as they move through the school, and of the progress of the school in terms of pupils of a particular age. Given that this data can be adjusted sensibly to take account of differences in intake, particularly in small schools where differences in the cohort can be significant (for example, a school taking in less than 50 pupils per year can experience major variations in the baselines of the pupils entering: the arrival of five highly achieving pupils can make a difference of 10% in outcomes, schools can build up a reliable picture of their progress in providing effectively for their pupils.

An essential element of assessment and evaluation at pupil level is the development of skills and processes by which the pupils evaluate their own progress with rigour and objectivity. Evidence shows that many pupils will set themselves more challenging (but still realistic) goals than their teachers. Pupils who set themselves lower targets can be worked with so that their expectations of their ability rise. Portfolios of pupils' work demonstrate their capabilities, and can positively affect self-esteem. Schools need systems and processes which enable pupils to carry out these 'self-assessments'. The processes of review which involve teachers and pupils in discussions of progress are valuable in several ways: they encourage pupils to analyse their progress, to use more sophisticated and technical language for a practical purpose, to discuss their progress more openly at home and to take greater responsibility for their own learning. There is evidence from a number of studies that this, coupled with close monitoring of individual pupils' progress, is an important feature of schools which cater well for children from ethnic minority backgrounds.

These processes enable pupils to set targets for themselves and be aware of their progress compared with pupils in other schools; they enable parents to form a better view of their child's progress; schools can set targets for themselves as institutions and with individual pupils; they enable schools to identify priorities for improvement and target their resources accordingly; they can help schools to identify where and why they have been successful in raising standards. These factors are discussed in more detail below.

2.2 Teachers and teaching
The quality of teaching is a key element of the overall quality of education, especially for ethnic minority children. The extent to which teachers

- are interculturally skilled

- are able to demonstrate to children that they recognise and value their cultural, faith and linguistic heritage

- can help to develop their pupils' mother tongues as well as their second or additional language

- use language or languages very well

- understand the theory and practice of language acquisition

- have high expectations of all pupils

- have excellent professional skills

is a major determinant of pupils' progress. These special but essential competences place major demands on teachers working with pupils from heritages other than their own, and this ought to be recognised in arrangements for career progression according to negotiated agreements between teachers and their employers. It is essential that schools which face additional challenges have access to teachers who have the required skills. Education systems have to respond to this challenge: working is more demanding in some schools than in others and ways have to be found of attracting and retaining some of the best teachers to schools which present additional challenges.

Does initial teacher training take account of the needs of pupils from different cultural, faith and linguistic backgrounds? Experience suggests that teachers are too often emerging from initial teacher training without the knowledge, skills, understanding and attitudes needed for successful work in multicultural schools, particularly in regard to a multi-level approach.

DIECEC sees much excellent work in schools which employ skilled bilingual or multilingual teachers and other staff from the ethnic minority communities represented in the school. Such teachers are invaluable if the school is to reflect the culture and values of the pupils and parents. The staff in any school must be skilled and professional in their work with the pupils. Employing staff from the same cultural backgrounds as the children becomes more difficult where the school serves a highly diverse population and the few children from a cultural background not reflected in the staff can be particularly marginalised. What matters most is whether staff are interculturally skilled, have high expectations of pupils and can help children to develop both their mother tongue and their second or additional language.

The importance of evaluating teaching processes

Self-evaluation and evaluation of teaching processes should be integral to school-level evaluation. Headteachers need to be involved in evaluation at classroom level and to facilitate effective professional dialogue with and between teachers. There should be strong elements of self-evaluation, peer observation and co-operation between teachers. DIECEC has considerable evidence that teacher action research programmes, in which teachers actively develop their methodologies and approaches in partnership with each other and within an open but rigorous system of classroom evaluation, enhance professional development and school effectiveness. Developing new approaches to teaching and learning, building on and sharing different practices schools can, in partnership, greatly assist this process, as can education advisory services.

The process of evaluation with teachers should cover a range of areas: classroom management, interaction with pupils, intercultural skills, teaching or instructional skills, levels of expectation, assessment processes, quality and quantity of pupils' work and, for ethnic minority pupils, the other areas set out at the start of this section. Video can also be useful. Teachers can see themselves and others at work and can discuss their teaching with their headteacher and colleagues, ideally as an an integral part of professional development. Videos can also be used for specific training activities and one-way screens have proved especially effective in developing teaching skills.

2.3 *Parents*

Parents are key partners in the education of children. The theme of Engaging Parents as Prime Educators (Section Four, Theme D), describes some of the many ways in which schools and cities can work effectively with parents, recognising the skills, knowledge and enthusiasms which they can bring to the school and the education of their children. Schools also need to

- make effective initial contact and build the confidence of parents

- provide or ensure access to additional education and training opportunities for them

- ensure that parents understand the school system and their child's progress

- enable them to support their children's education at home

- actively involve them in the school

Some cities manage such a curriculum for working with parents at whole city level. This is described in more detail in Theme D. Schools need to be prepared to measure themselves or be evaluated on how parents feel empowered in helping their children to achieve highly.

- is the school seen as open and welcoming to parents?

- does it recognise the potential and actual contributions of parents to their children's education?

- does the school recognise parents as the prime educators of their children?

- how does the school actively engage parents in this role and help them to fulfil it?

- do parents feel well-informed about their children's progress and understand how their progress compares with that of children in other schools?

Schools and cities can use certain key indicators to evaluate parents' contribution to their children's education. These include:

- attendance of parents at consultation meetings about their child's progress

- the number and range of parents providing additional educational opportunities for children, and the quality and diversity of these opportunities

- the proportion of parents themselves involved in learning activities

- the levels of parents' formal education and training qualifications

- measures of parents' attitudes to the school

- parents' understanding about the education system in which their children learn

- the percentage of parents involved in work in the school on a voluntary or paid basis

- (at the appropriate ages) the number of parents who read with their children

Proxy indicators include returns from letters sent home and pupils' response to homework. Attendance and punctuality can also be proxy indicators for the value parents place on education.

Schools and cities should use information about parents to enhance parental engagement. It is not enough for schools to expect or hope that parents will become involved – they have to be welcoming and pro-active. Schools and cities should decide where their priorities for work with parents lie: in many cases it will be in activities before the parents feel ready to become more involved with the school.

DIECEC has found that engaging parents and working with them is a key factor in raising pupils' achievement, especially those from ethnic minority and disadvantaged backgrounds. Engaging parents is a vital feature of the multi-level approach, as it addresses a key component of the triangle of home, school and community. So it warrants careful evaluation and the identification of priorities for action.

2.4 Schools

Schools must have reliable and valid information about the effectiveness of both their processes and their outcomes of education. They also need reliable information about the pupils, including details of their previous levels of achievement at the point where they first enter school, and, as indicated above, about parents. To reiterate: the notion of a 'baseline' is important to all schools and not just the first school attended. Issues regarding the generation and uses of data and other evidence are set out in section 2.1 above and in the introduction to this section of the Handbook.

Data and qualitative information are best used in a cyclical way over the year.

- As soon as possible (probably in the early Autumn), review and analyse the outcomes of the previous year's work for the pupils and teachers' evaluations of the effectiveness of the curriculum.

- Work with teachers, departments and individual pupils to set targets for the current year and beyond, reviewing performance against any previously agreed targets.

- Identify what specifically needs to be done to address underperformance; detail these in action plans and establish timescales for review and evaluation.

- Keep the targets and the action plans under review and keep to the timescales agreed.

- Check out progress at suitable times (for example, overall progress in reading after about four months).

- Towards the end of the year, check progress on the implementation and outcomes of the action plans – you may have to wait for the more objective data arising from assessment and examination results, but the effectiveness of action plans can be assessed sooner.

It is vital to identify differences in performance at an early stage and between different ethnic groups. DIECEC has learned that pupils cannot simply be described as 'Asian' or 'African and Caribbean' and their achievement levels lumped together as though they were a single homogeneous group. At both school and city or education system levels, it is essential to have a clear view of the performance of particular groups within these broader definitions (describing Pakistani pupils from Mirpur as 'Asian' is akin to describing Dutch-speaking pupils as 'European'). More detailed but relevant analyses are essential – for example, if a group from a particular background is performing well, the school needs to know why and how, and compare their experience to that of other groups which are still underachieving.

The section above on pupils and groups of pupils emphasises the importance of their evaluating their own progress. The close monitoring and support of individual pupils, especially as they grow older, is an important complementary factor in maintaining progress and raising achievement. Where pupils can see that they are making progress, where monitoring processes convince pupils that the school and individual teachers are interested in them as individuals (as opposed to simply holding them to account), and where monitoring results in swift action when necessary, ethnic minority (and other) pupils tend to make better progress. Schools need to build these features into their overall evaluation processes. This positive attention to the progress and achievements of ethnic minority pupils may well be a key determinant of their success in school.

Nearby schools should pool their information, especially about parents and the community. The value of this can be considerable – data from different sources will normally give a more accurate picture. Schools will see that they face similar challenges especially in relation to scaffolding children's and young people's education outside school, and may be able and willing to pool their resources and work together. Their city and/or educational authority should support these initiatives and provide the schools with relevant information, for example, data arising from a census, including up-to-date socio-economic information. This centralised data can also help schools if it identifies trends and probable future changes in the population of the area they serve.

Schools may find it useful to work with their close neighbours, but they should also work with schools further away which have a similar pupil profile but are achieving different outcomes. ICT enables schools to link with each other, even in different countries. Schools in different European countries serving similar or indeed different and diverse populations have found it valuable to exchange experiences, work together on better solutions to challenges, learn from and with each other, organise direct links between pupils ... DIECEC would say this but it is true. And to develop better understanding of the educational and cultural traditions schools, cities and education systems do well to link with schools and other organisations (for example, teacher training institutions) in the countries of origin of their pupils. Several DIECEC cities and schools have imaginative links of this kind and they have proved to be mutually advantageous.

DIECEC's experience suggests that the answers to so-called 'intractable' underachievement of ethnic minority pupils lie not only within the walls of the schools and with issues such as the quality of teaching, however important. They lie also in the existence or lack of an effective scaffolding for children's education at home and in the community, and the success of the school in reflecting the diversity of values and culture of these contexts. Using a small number of simple, reliable and valid indicators and relevant data about home and the community is as important as using internal indicators of quality. This is where schools which have developed effective internal evaluation processes as outlined above should move next if they are to develop a rigorous multi-level approach to evaluation.

2.5 *Cities and whole education systems*

Cities and education systems at local, provincial or national level can operate as external evaluators for schools, working alongside schools' self-evaluation processes – generally through local education advisory services. Schools need a 'critical friend' to challenge where appropriate and also to support and spread good practice. They should provide high-quality data about the performance of the school in relation to other schools and groups of pupils locally, nationally and, increasingly, transnationally. This data is crucial to prevent schools from becoming divorced from the reality of achievement levels elsewhere, to enable them to plan and evaluate effectively and to support their overall strategy for improvement.

The processes and educational outcomes for pupils from ethnic minorities, based on reliable, pupil-level data, must be evaluated at city or whole local system level. Only at this level can trends across a whole city or a whole cohort of pupils be identified. Major successful initiatives which have raised the achievement levels of pupils from ethnic minorities within DIECEC cities have resulted from such city-level evaluation. The schools, cities and education systems all benefit from exchanging pupil-level and aggregated data on the one hand, and aggregated city and system-level data on the other. Cities cannot fulfil their role without pupil-level data; schools need system-level information to inform their development.

Cities therefore need access to anonymised pupil-level data from schools and others involved in education so they can analyse the information and identify priorities for action at city level. There may be implications of these analyses for many areas of professional and voluntary activity within a city, and for overall city policy in relation to young people. But the cities themselves should be evaluated on the basis of their role.

Section 8 sets this out: providing clear vision and leadership, providing access to additional resources, providing specific support, establishing and maintaining multi-level partnerships and carrying out their part of evaluation. Cities should be evaluated against indicators which relate to these roles, by a university or other professional research and evaluation body. The proposed DIECEC Research Project, DEURP (DIECEC European Research Project) is designed to put in place such evaluation systems at city level. They must also construct their own system of indicators for evaluation or, better still, have it undertaken by an external body. These indicators need to cover, at city and education system levels, the three contexts of learning at school, at home and in the community.

It is important to focus on indicators of outcomes for pupils; indicators of process are important (especially those relating to the quality of teaching, engagement of parents, involvement in additional educational activities etc.). Indicators of levels of provision or input are of more limited value. Having a pre-school place, but experiencing a negative start as a result of contact with an untrained or unqualified 'teacher' (as can be the case) does nothing for the self-esteem and achievement levels of any child. So focus on the outcomes for the pupils, within the broad definition of achievement to which DIECEC subscribes.

Case Study of a Multi-level Approach: School improvement in Birmingham

City of Birmingham LEA:
Suraj Masson, DIECEC City Representative
John Hill, Head of Research and Statistics Branch (R&S)

Tel: 00 44 121 303 8840
Fax: 00 44 121 303 8844
E-Mail: jhill@lea.birmingham.gov.uk

Birmingham has a school population of about 176,500 of which roughly 40% are of ethnic minority origin, mainly from Pakistan, India, the Caribbean and Bangladesh. The LEA has a Research and Statistics Branch which collects, aggregates, analyses and uses educational data to inform schools' and the LEA's work on school improvement and raising standards. It leads and co-ordinates this work in close liaison with other services, especially the Birmingham Advisory and Support Service. It works with pupil-level data about attainment, attendance and other key indicators. Analyses are carried out according to ethnicity, gender, socio-economic and other features of pupils' backgrounds. Data is held on pupil performance from entry to school at age five through to age eighteen.

The R and S Branch receives information from schools and national sources to identify, analyse and compare assessments of pupils on entry to school (baseline assessment) and at the end of each Key Stage of their education – at age 7, 11, 14 and 16. It also collects data about progression to further education. The analyses are used to determine priorities for action at school and city levels, to agree targets for individual schools and aggregate these to determine or reflect targets for the city.

The R and S Branch works with schools on value-added measures by helping them to identify the value they are adding to children's education compared with what they should add on the basis of reliable data about the children's previous attainment. Analyses of the socio-economic backgrounds of children have also enabled the Branch to identify schools across the city with very similar pupil populations and for these schools to look together at any significant differences in performance.

In terms of the ethnic minority children in Birmingham, the R and S Branch is able to provide analyses which identify how different groups are performing in relation to each other, to identify issues (for example, the performance of boys of African and Caribbean origin) and suggest ways forward.

The Research and Statistics Branch aims

- to provide aggregated data and data analyses which can be set alongside qualitative information about schools to compare performance, identify priorities for action and set targets

- to support schools with their own analyses and enable them to develop their expertise in using educational data for internal management purposes

- to enable schools and the city to differentiate between the performance of pupils from different backgrounds, including race and gender, so as to identify, take and evaluate action

- to assist schools with the management and development of data so that they can monitor and evaluate their own performance with increasing effectiveness both in absolute terms and how they compare with similar schools

Data on pupil performance is collected from schools electronically or using optical mark readers (OMRs – a system of reading information from sheets completed in schools). These data are then analysed using a range of commercially available software. Reports are prepared using tables and graphs to illustrate trends in performance and comparisons between the relative performance of groups of pupils, broken down by gender, ethnicity and socio-economic background. One example of analysis concerned the impact of nursery education on children's achievements when they start school. It showed that nursery education improved children's performance in literacy and numeracy and was particularly effective in raising the achievement levels of pupils with English as an additional language.

This development is characterised by:

- a city-wide, whole education system approach to managing and using data for the purposes of school improvement

- a means of ensuring that the city and schools can identify issues relating to the achievement levels of different ethnic minority groups and respond accordingly

What has been learned?

- There are significant differences in achievement levels between different groups of pupils when analysed by ethnic group, mother tongue and gender. This helps in targeting resources and support services.

- These data-based analyses produce fairer assessment of school standards. By analysing results in context and identifying the value added by schools to their pupils' achievement levels, different children's starting points can be taken into account.

- Schools making the most progress can be identified and the reasons can be deduced and good practice shared between schools.

- Using data in these ways helps teachers and schools to identify strengths and weaknesses in their performance and that of their pupils, to set targets for improvement and to monitor progress.

Main Outcomes

- pupils gain in self-esteem because their achievements are recognised in relation to their previous best performance

- standards of literacy and numeracy have risen significantly in many schools

- teachers are better able to diagnose pupils' relative strengths and weaknesses

- teachers can monitor the effects of specific classroom interventions with individuals and groups of pupils

- schools can interpret the outcomes achieved by their pupils in the context of their school population and of other similar schools

- teachers and schools are better able to set targets and monitor progress

- schools can identify and monitor the value they are adding to pupils' education

- parents receive better information about the progress their children are making

- the LEA can monitor standards, identify trends, support schools better and tailor its support to clearly identified needs.

Implications for In-Service Training

- The staff of schools' and cities' education systems need training in the appropriate uses of educational data for planning, management and school improvement purposes. Such training should be provided in the framework of a supportive approach to school improvement.

- LEA advisory staff require training in the processes which schools and the city/LEA need to use to make the most effective use of data. They also need to be able to evaluate how schools are using data and advise them about the most effective ways of doing this in relation to the improvement of their performance. They should also be trained to help schools to interpret their data, identify issues and design appropriate action.

A video showing how three primary schools have used pupil achievement data to set targets and monitor pupils' progress is available from the city contributors.

SECTION TWO
MULTI-LEVEL WORKING IN CITIES
AND WHOLE EDUCATION SYSTEMS

This Handbook emphasises the importance for the achievement levels of ethnic minority children and young people of effective scaffolding for their education and learning in the contexts of school, home and community. This scaffolding can be erected through the actions of schools and others, supported by their city, local authority, education system and other agencies. Work in the DIECEC cities has led to firm conclusions:

- schools cannot be expected to put effective scaffolding in place for learning in these three contexts without considerable moral and practical support

- it is an ineffective use of resources for schools to act individually, especially in relation to provision of additional learning opportunities

- where a co-ordinated approach is put in place, schools can be a major force for community regeneration

- many schools need practical help if they are to form key partnerships, for example with parents and the local community or communities.

Cities and those responsible for leading and administering education systems can assist schools greatly in establishing this scaffolding and developing their key partnerships. While some schools may be able to do this on their own, for a whole education system to produce better outcomes for ethnic minority children a consistent and co-ordinated approach across schools is necessary. Cities are in a unique position to do this, and it is one of the ways in which they can add considerable value to the education of children and young people.

Adding value to education

In the experience of the DIECEC Network, the cities' role in constructing an effective support system for learners can be summed up as follows:

- to provide leadership on the issue of multi-level, whole community approaches to education. This involves developing, co-ordinating, communicating and promoting a vision of education which has schools at its heart but which reaches out to and engages the whole community by co-ordinating and incorporating different views from within communities and organisations. The city needs to provide leadership which enables a clear consensus to emerge about a way forward. As stressed elsewhere in the Handbook, this is a framework, not a blueprint. Where cities do not have a statutory responsibility for the school system, they need to develop this vision in partnership with the authorities which have this responsibility and with the schools

• within this, to promote and support in practical ways the development of excellent education in schools of high standards, of learning in the three contexts of home, school and community and of the empowerment of parents and communities. Cities and education systems can work more effectively with schools to engage parents in their role as the actual or potential prime educators of their children because this is known to raise achievement levels

• to provide models of multi-level working. Cities and education systems can, for example, restructure themselves so that they present a more coherent and co-ordinated image and way of working, integrating functions which support education and learning. And they can develop approaches to policy – for example, integrated policies on the education and social welfare of children and young people – which reflect the multi-level approach

• to provide directly or act as a doorway to additional resources and practical support from a variety of sources, which can underpin the provision of effective learning opportunities in the contexts of home, school and community. Many of the experiences within the DIECEC cities suggest that it is not necessarily shortage of resources which hinders progress but that existing resources are used less than effectively because they are inadequately co-ordinated

• therefore, to put in place mechanisms for the co-ordination of resources at city level within public, private and voluntary sector services which affect or can contribute to scaffolding children's and young people's education effectively in the three contexts

• to provide directly, or co-ordinate, positive and developmental mechanisms for evaluating progress of communities and schools so that they have reliable comparative information. This enables all the partners concerned to form a realistic view of their progress and the achievement levels of their learners so that they can identify what actions will help them to improve further

• to ensure that services which exist to support children directly do so in partnership with schools and in ways which schools find helpful; even if this involves challenging schools over how they work with individual pupils, this has to be done in ways which help the school.

The city's or education system's role in promoting, leading, supporting and helping to evaluate whole community, multi-level approaches can be illustrated by the following diagram:

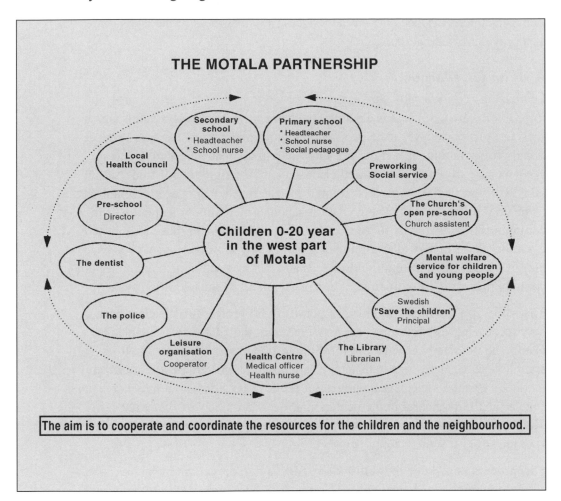

THE MOTALA PARTNERSHIP

Children 0-20 year in the west part of Motala

Secondary school
* Headteacher
* School nurse

Primary school
* Headteacher
* School nurse
* Social pedagogue

Local Health Council

Pre-school Director

The dentist

The police

Leisure organisation Cooperator

Health Centre Medical officer Health nurse

The Library Librarian

Swedish "Save the children" Principal

Mental welfare service for children and young people

The Church's open pre-school Church assistent

Preworking Social service

The aim is to cooperate and coordinate the resources for the children and the neighbourhood.

Cities' and local authorities' responsibilities for the formal system of schooling vary greatly across DIECEC's membership; some have almost total respon-sibility; some have responsibility for aspects of educational provision; some have no responsibility for schools but a more general role in providing educa-tional opportunities which complement the school system; some have direct responsibilities for aspects of the system but share other responsibilities with governors or managers of schools, who themselves have discrete respon-sibilities.

Whatever the context, it is the cities which reap the rewards or have to cope with the outcomes of educational provision in the city. If children fail in the system, it is the city which has to respond to the consequences, often at considerable cost. If young people are marginalised, the ill effects are felt by cities. So cities not only have responsibilities, they have a clear social and economic interest in seeking to ensure effective scaffolding for children's and young people's education. This interest is the same, in the longer term, regardless of the city's status as a provider of education.

A vision for education

Leadership, co-ordination and support – as opposed to power, control and imposition – are key. There is a parallel to be drawn with schools; schools which seek to exert power over their pupil communities and control them and educational provision through a rigid and authoritarian approach are unlikely to succeed, particularly in a multicultural environment. The rigidity will find itself at odds with the flexible approach required for catering for the needs of children from very different backgrounds. But a school which simply responds to the community is unlikely to succeed either, because it will not have established common cause or provided a rationale for the way it works, nor will it have played a lead role in integrating the needs and cultures within its community or communities with the requirements and expectations of the education system.

The same applies at city level; their political and professional leaders have a duty to develop and communicate a vision about the education available. This vision should clearly articulate a locally-interpreted version of the multi-level approach, particularly for disadvantaged communities and ethnic minority communities. But the same caveat applies for schools: be clear about the ends, but enable flexibility in local implementation. Provide a framework, not a blueprint. The city can play an important role in raising the aspirations, expectations and outcomes for all young people.

This process must value the skills, knowledge and understanding which exist in all its communities and not emphasise problems, high levels of disadvantage and the need for more resources to combat them. Cities which take a positive view of their and their citizens' abilities to overcome such situations have a far greater chance of success and are more likely to attract additional resources.

Support for educational quality

Some cities direct specific resources to support schools in improving the quality of education and the standards they achieve, generally where cities function as local authorities with responsibility for statutory schooling. Education advisory services support educational quality through development work with schools, in-service training, monitoring and evaluation and support for priorities such as basic skills, teaching quality, management and leadership of schools.

Cities which do not have this formal responsibility or the resources to provide such support can still contribute to the quality of education in schools, as well as to the multi-level approach. For example, several DIECEC cities co-ordinate additional educational activities which enhance young people's learning opportunities and which schools can access for their pupils. Cities also run or co-ordinate specific projects with schools, for example on engaging parents or on providing specific support for vulnerable children.

The issue for cities is to ensure that these support activities address the needs of ethnic minority children and young people and, where they involve learning activities, ensure that these correspond to the needs of the pupils and that they can access them. More about this question of access can be found in Theme I. Pathways to Further and Higher Education, Training and Employment.

Access to resources

Cities are in a position to bring together different sources of funding and different providers of educational and recreational activities. By working with these partners – foundations and trusts, other organisations and people within the communities served by schools – sensitising them if necessary to the needs of communities and promoting the multi-level approach, cities can enable schools to access additional resources and/or run activities. Individual schools benefit most when this facilitative function operates comprehensively and consistently across the city – meaning that the other services and organisations involved will also be operating a multi-level approach and not be restricted to pockets of the organisation which work with individual schools.

Co-ordination with other organisations and providers

Cities also have a coordination function, attracting to schools other services and organisations interested in education, training and the welfare of pupils. Cities also need to work with these services and organisations to embed the concept of multi-level working in their management structures and processes. Leaving individual schools to work with representatives of organisations and services on a one-off basis can cause problems for them, especially if the management of the service does not understand what is happening. Positive intervention from the city at strategic level with these services and agencies is essential. Some such co-operation already exists, but mostly over vulnerable children and child protection issues and with the services most involved (social services, psychological service, health services, education welfare). Cities and education authorities need to work hard at constructing positive partnerships with other providers of educational and recreational activities and at co-ordinating these with statutory schooling processes.

Co-ordination of groups of schools to develop multi-level working

Cities and education systems are well-placed to promote the value of groups of schools working together, especially over the scaffolding of education at home and in the community. Even where education systems tend to set schools in competition, there are examples of groups or 'families' of schools working together, at the instigation or with the support of the city, for the greater good of the whole educational community. How this can be done and the benefits gained are described on page 59.

A multi-level approach to evaluation

Finally, cities have a role role to ensure a good framework for evaluation based on qualitative and quantitative information. The rationale for this and some of the processes involved are reported on page 00 and in a case study. Cities need to see their role in evaluation as part of a developmental approach which benefits schools, parents, pupils and communities as well as the city itself. Cities with no formal responsibility for the education system can work with schools and others on the evaluation of the other elements of the scaffolding of learning and provide feedback indicating where improvements can be made and providing agreed support where necessary.

Case studies

The following case studies illustrate how the DIECEC cities are responding to the challenges of these roles. Some of them are at the stage of developing one or more aspects of the role; others are now in a position to adopt a more comprehensive strategy. Some have altered their structures and approaches to policy and thus changed practice, whilst others have started with changes in practice which have led to greater integration of policies – with possible impact on structures at city level. What the case studies have in common is their appreciation of how the city can make a major difference to ethnic minority pupils' educational attainment. Other cities keen to adopt a multi-level approach and to work with the schools serving their children may wish to consider where to begin. There are many possible starting points and no single 'correct' line of approach.

Case Study 2.1

The role of CD/LEI (Centro Documentazione/Laboratorio per un Educazione Interculturale) in developing intercultural education in Bologna

Contact: Miriam Traversi (Director, CD/LEI)

Tel: 00 39 051 340 856

Fax: 00 39 051 397 306

E-mail: Miriam.Traversi@comune.bologna.it

Website: http://www.miriam.traversi/comunedibologna/it

CD/LEI is a centre for intercultural education in Bologna, supported by the Provincial Education Authority, the Municipality of Bologna, the Department of Education of the University of Bologna, the Education Department of the Province of Bologna and National Trades Unions. Representatives of these first four organisations, all of which have a key role in education in the city and region of Bologna, form a management committee to oversee the work of the Centre. This support structure for the Centre illustrates multi-level working, as close co-operation is needed between the partners in the Centre's financial support, its promotion and steering. The Centre works with schools, teachers, students and any other people and organisations interested in intercultural education. It co-operates closely with a number of NGOs (Non-Governmental Organisations) with an interest in intercultural education, and with the Bologna Immigrants Forum, an organisation which brings together representatives of the different minority groups in the city and region.

CD/LEI is DIECEC's main partner in Bologna, participating in several projects and leading the 'Open Sesame' project, which is establishing mobile libraries of intercultural materials and reading books for ethnic minority and other pupils in five DIECEC cities. CD/LEI also works in other European Projects concerning, for example, the education of gypsy and traveller children and parents.

CD/LEI has a Director and administrative support. It can call on local teachers and friends of the Centre willing to undertake work on a voluntary basis. CD/LEI's main role is as a Documentation Centre, but it provides a wide range of services to teachers and schools, including:

- providing materials to support teaching in intercultural education and developing methodologies which support an intercultural approach in classrooms

- translating materials for teachers and students into Italian

- translating information and other materials for parents of ethnic minority origin into thirteen different community languages

- providing access to the work of the DIECEC projects in which CD/LEI and Bologna are directly involved, as well as to the other projects within the Network, and other European projects

- a book-loan service to teachers, students, volunteers, researchers etc

- counselling and advice to schools at local, provincial, regional and national levels (for example, with schools in Rome, Pisa and Reggio Calabria) on the pedagogical and technical organisation of courses and possible lecturers for local events; copies of the courses and programmes run by CD/LEI are sent to other organisations for them to use

- in-service training for teachers, other professionals and others such as volunteers working in NGOs based on successful intercultural work in projects and in local schools and other organisations

- other practical and moral support for people working locally in the field of intercultural education

- support for the Bologna Immigrants Forum

- creating internet pages on the Centre's documentation and dissemination activities.

As well as being a multi-level organisation in the way in which it is established and supported, CD/LEI also works at many levels within the city of Bologna, giving support and advice to schools, teachers, other professionals (for example, the Social Services of Bologna), NGOs, parents and community organisations.

CD/LEI aims to promote and develop intercultural education in Bologna so that children, young people and families from ethnic minority backgrounds can achieve greater educational success and enjoy a better quality of life.

CD/LEI engages in a wide range of activities but its method of working is consistently through local, regional, national and European networking. It offers a wide range of materials, advice and in-service training opportunities, and works with a wide range of organisations.

CD/LEI illustrates how effective multi-level working can be in promoting and developing intercultural education and improving the education of children and young people from ethnic minorities. The small permanent staff of the centre are able to undertake a range of work which would be impossible without a multi-level approach. The multi-level approach is also evident in the activities it carries out, for example in promoting and providing practical support for schools in engaging with parents, and in its work with NGOs.

What has been learned?
- intercultural education has to be promoted and supported in cities through a multi-level approach

- teachers and schools need solid support and encouragement, especially in their early dealings with ethnic minority children and families, including considerable practical advice

- a multi-level organisation, supported by mainline city, regional and academic organisations, can achieve much with relatively few resources

- it is important to engage with work being carried out nationally and on a European level as well as locally

Main Outcomes

- teachers have been engaged by the work of CD/LEI in an active involvement in the provision of training courses

- teachers provide a valuable source of feedback to CD/LEI to help it to develop its services

- increasing numbers of teachers are developing specialist knowledge and expertise in working with ethnic minority pupils and their families

- parents have become more informed about and involved in the education of their children through personal counselling at CD/LEI and being given information about the school system

- home-school liaison arrangements and contacts have been greatly improved

- pupils benefit from all of the above, including working with better informed and motivated teachers and having better support from their parents; the achievement levels and attendance records of ethnic minority children have improved as a result

- increasing numbers of schools are better informed about the policies and practices they can use to cater effectively for ethnic minority pupils and more now participate in CD/LEI's activities

- schools are responding positively to the sensitive and sensible ways in which CD/LEI works with them as a result of both pilot projects run in schools and the training and other activities organised by the Centre

- the whole community benefits from CD/LEI's growing activities through its multilevel approach. There are better understandings between different communities, and a wider appreciation of the empowering effects of good education.

Implications for in-service training

- Each local area or region requires an organisation which can provide in-service training in a way which raises important issues in a sensitive and sensible way which enables schools to make progress without feeling de-skilled.

- Ensure that there is sufficient capacity to provide in-service for the wide range of teachers and other people who want or need it. CD/LEI's address book includes over 1,400 teachers and 600 other people (including volunteers). Over 1,400 teachers per year receive some training from a range of four or five different programmes related to intercultural education and raising achievement. CD/LEI achieves a tremendous amount with very few resources.

- the range of people who need or ask for in-service, including people from other city services, other organisations and students as well as headteachers and teachers in schools, is growing rapidly. Training arrangements need to ensure that all the people who need training have access to it, and that a comprehensive programme is available, supported by good materials.

Case Study 2.2

Policy for ethnic minority pupils in Helsinki

City of Helsinki Ulla Kauppinen, Riitta Veinio,
2. Contact telephone and fax, e-mail address of contributor(s):
Tel: ** 358 9310 86870
Fax: ** 358 9310 86490
E-mail: riita.veinio@edu.hel.fi

Helsinki has a growing population of ethnic minority children and young people, including pupils from Russia, Estonia and Somalia. The Finnish constitution and legislation deriving from it require Local Authorities in Finland to make provision for ethnic minority people so that they have equality of opportunity to succeed and can enjoy the same quality of life as Finns.

Helsinki has a clear policy of making particular arrangements for the reception, induction, education and training of ethnic minority children and young people, including those who arrive during the later stages of compulsory education. Finland has two main languages – Finnish and Swedish – and a third language is spoken by the Sami people who live mainly in the North of the country. Finnish law is consequently based on the needs of a diverse population and the policies relating to ethnic minorities are based on principles which are fundamental to the constitution (basic law) of the Finnish State.

Schools in Helsinki have delegated powers to manage their own resources and the city authority (the Education Committee and the Helsinki City Education Department) works in partnership with the schools to strive for the most effective arrangements for education and training for ethnic minority children and young people.

Aims of the policy

*   to secure equality of opportunity and equal access to education, training and employment for people from ethnic minorities

*   to provide this so that people from diverse backgrounds can enjoy an equally high quality of life

*   to ensure that arrangements are in place to meet the diverse educational, social and cultural needs of ethnic minorities

*   to ensure that training is available to employees (city staff, headteachers, teachers), in collaboration with appropriate training institutions (for example, the University of Helsinki) to help them meet the needs of ethnic minority pupils

*   to recognise the rights and responsibilities of all parents and to support them in their role as prime educators of their children.

In practice, the policy is aimed at addressing:

- parents' and pupils' knowledge of the education system and of their rights and responsibilities by providing information in different ethnic minority languages

- parents' and pupils' need to acquire Finnish as a second or additional language as rapidly as possible, together with a knowledge and understanding of Finnish culture

- the background of ethnic minority children by reflecting their own culture in schools

- the particular needs of individual young people of all ages, through programmes and courses designed to enable them to progress from their current position to recognised levels of qualification

- the need to provide effective scaffolding for children's learning outside normal school hours and before the age of statutory schooling.

This development is characterised by:

- a whole city approach to meeting the needs of ethnic minority children and young people through clear policies, based on legislative requirements and resulting in a wide range of additional provision

- a commitment through the policy to making a positive response to diversity and to the needs of children and young people from ethnic minority backgrounds

- specific actions and resources to meet the needs of ethnic minority children, including the provision of a structured framework for teaching Finnish as a second language and additional resources for teaching and learning Finnish and for mother tongue teaching

- a specific focus on providing additional education and training opportunities for young people who arrive in Helsinki in the late years of compulsory schooling and often without recognised qualifications or a level of education commensurate with their age – this includes specific opportunities within the vocational training system.

What has been learned?

- A clear policy is essential on issues such as provision of information, specific resources to address needs including second language and mother tongue development if developments are to be coherent, co-ordinated and sustained.

- Children from ethnic minority backgrounds need considerable support at home and in their community for their education if they are to succeed at similar levels to their peers.

- Schools can have a major impact on scaffolding children's education in the contexts of home, school and community – but only if they have the support of a wide range of people and organisations plus a clear policy framework provided by the city and the national education system.

Implications for in-service training:

*   City staff and those responsible for policy and its implementation through city services need training in the needs and backgrounds of different ethnic minority groups.

*   Teachers and other staff working in schools need training in the linguistic, cultural, faith and other aspects of background of ethnic minority pupils, and how to respond appropriately.

*   Headteachers need training in how to support pupils from ethnic minorities and work effectively with their parents so that their children's education is well-supported outside as well as inside school.

*   Cities and those responsible for different parts of the education system need to work with the providers of initial and in-service training to ensure that the issues of intercultural achievement are addressed in training programmes and that there is a clear understanding of the links between intercultural education and the achievement levels of all pupils and especially those from ethnic minority backgrounds.

Case Study 2.3

Multi-Level Education System in T1, Linkoping, Sweden

City of Linkoping, Snezana Nero, Mary Dahlin, Birgitta Dahlgren
Tel: 00 46 13 206 966
Fax: 00 46 13 205 817
E-mail: birgitta.dahlgren@ti.linkoping.se

T1 is a former army facility which became surplus to requirements. It was within the city boundary and the city council took a decision to create a new district which would attract a balanced population in terms of the age, socio-economic circumstances and ethnic origin of the people living there, along with other factors (for example, a representative number of people with disabilities).

The city decided to adopt a multi-level approach to educational provision in the area. Building on the Swedish tradition of integrated community facilities, five primary school units were built in T1, all under the supervision of one headteacher. Other services which relate closely to the educational needs of children in the area (social services, youth services) also have bases within the area to enable co-operation and multi-level working. Additional learning opportunities for children are provided after school. The school units in T1 serves a total primary-aged pupil population of 277, amongst whom approximately 15% receive tuition in Swedish as a second language.

A research project was carried out in T1 by the University of Linkoping, covering everything from the vision which underpins the area to the details of teaching methods. The T1 motto is: 'The Spirit of Community, Participation and Responsibility'. People moving into the area are invited to a meeting with the neighbours in their block or housing development and certain families are elected to take care of new neighbours and explain how the community functions. All those working in the area attend a course which gives information on what this motto means for the area. The local church is closely involved with the schools, offering in-school care free of charge for 80 minutes per week to all 8 year-old children. The church pays for two members of staff to do this work and parents may attend to check whether there is a religious aspect to it – there is not.

There is a local support group made up of a social worker, psychologist, representatives from the local health centre and from the schools and day care services, who work together and exchange information which will benefit families, children and individuals living in the area by ensuring a co-ordinated response to their needs.

The local health centre and church have been involved in setting up an 'open' meeting place for parents who are not eligible for child care facilities and this project has two members of staff paid for by the local authority (Linkopings Kommun). The local health centre has targeted the mothers of ethnic minority children through courses in cooking. The church also provides a meeting place for fathers and young men.

The spirit of community, participation and responsibility runs through all the activities organised in T1 and helps to ensure a multi-level approach to the support provided for children and families in many aspects of their lives, not just education. The multi-level approach to education is therefore reflected in other aspects of children's and young people's lives.

This development is characterised by:

- a multi-level approach to the provision of education and other services in a city district

- a focus on the needs of the whole child and a multi-level response to these needs through co-ordination of services

- a coherent philosophy of education applied throughout the area, underpinned by the role of the headteacher, who plays a lead role in developing multi-level working

- the headteacher has a budget which has to be used to provide statutory and additional educational and childcare facilities for all the children in T1

- the headteacher also has responsibility for the premises used by the various school classes and day-care facilities

- the headteacher has contacts with all the different organisations working in the area and, as they say in Swedish, is 'the spider in the web' of the organisation in T1.

Main outcomes and learning points

- running this system in T1 is more expensive than was anticipated when it was devised in the 1980s!

- the children in the area feel secure and are sure of their identity; they have a sense of belonging to their school and to the area

- children help each other and much peer education goes on which helps younger and older children to make progress

- the children learn to take responsibility for themselves and each other

- the teachers at the schools are used to working with other professionals and to working in teams; this concept of teamwork is now being introduced into Swedish schools generally

- the schools are frequently visited by other teachers and staff interested in how to develop a multi-disciplinary approach to supporting children and young people

- teachers from the schools give in-service courses about the approaches they use and their expertise is recognised.

Implications for in-service training

Teachers working in multi-level approaches need training in working with other professionals and may also need training in relating to parents from different cultural backgrounds.

- All staff working in T1 have been involved in training related to developing a 'learning organisation'. This has helped to develop the concept and practice of multi-agency working.

- All schools in Linkoping have been involved in Total Quality Management projects which have helped to improve the quality of education they provide.

Case Study 2.4

Structuring and organising education and related services: a multi-level approach

City of Odense, Denmark. Kirsten Wandall, Peter Steen Jensen.
Tel: ** 45 66 148 814 5101
Fax: ** 45 66 140 430
E-mail: KFW@odense.dk
Website: www.odense.dk

The City of Odense has a population of circa 189,000 of which 6.1% are from ethnic minority backgrounds. Since 1991/2 the city has been responsible for the provision of education up to the end of statutory schooling (normally age 15/16). All schools operate a system of local management, which means they manage their own resources, including curriculum resources, staffing and building maintenance. In 1993 a political decision was taken to focus specifically on childcare and youth within services provided by the city. A process of development and reorganisation of city services resulted in a structure of five departments. One of these – the Department for Education and Youth – has responsibility for

- education (kindergarten, primary and lower secondary)
- social Services
- youth services up to the age of 18
- leisure and recreation.

Most of the services which can play a major role in scaffolding children's and young people's education in schools, at home and in the community are thus grouped together in a single department of the City Council. All these services report within the same Committee of the Council.

Taxpayers in Denmark pay high national and local taxes – up to 60% of income – and this is reflected in legislation which requires city authorities to make a kindergarten place available to the children of any parents who ask for it. Local authorities also have to support local organisations (community associations, local activity groups) which set themselves up to provide community activities. There is a tradition in Denmark of people undertaking activities together in their community.

The restructuring of the city's services and committees reflects a multi-level approach to education. This was based on a political and professional understanding of the need to co-ordinate and create greater coherence between services focusing on the needs of children and young people. Although there is as yet no written Integrated Youth Policy, such a policy exists in terms of the functioning of the services and the committee.

The action plans developed by different services focus on groups of people of different ages, including infants and adolescents. The city has five identified areas, each with its District Committee focusing on the needs of children and young people. Important partners in the process of constructing an effective support system (scaffolding) of education at local level sit on these committees, including headteachers and senior social services staff. Some committees might be called community committees or boards. Each committee has four members – the head of a kindergarten, the head of a school, the head of a 'Youth School' (Ungdomsskole) and a social welfare officer.

Senior staff from the Department responsible for education, social services, youth services and leisure and recreation went out to schools and forums in the different Districts to promote the multi-level approach. They set out to promote the inclusion within all schools' development and action plans of three foci:

- progression of children and young people through the education system and into further and higher education, training and employment

- horizontal links between schools and other providers of educational, leisure and youth services with a view to providing effective scaffolding for learning in and outside school

- breadth and balance in the education of children and young people.

Aims of the organisation of education and related services in Odense

The main aim of the reorganisation was to improve the quality of education and the life chances of children and young people whatever their background, by setting up a multi-level approach to their education at schools, at home and in their community. Further aims were:

- to be able to address the needs of more children at an earlier stage

- to establish local mechanisms to identify and meet needs

- to improve the flexibility of services and ensure a co-ordinated response to families and children facing particular difficulties

- to ensure greater flexibility of funding so that resources could be targeted more effectively and transferred quickly from one area to another when required.

The restructuring of services came about as a result of political and professional realisation that individual services tended to work in isolation and that a better response to needs, a far more coherent effect and better value for money could be achieved by co-ordinating the work of services relating to the needs of particular client groups and placing them within a committee structure which could maintain a comprehensive oversight for particular groups of people.

The District Committees are intended to play an important role in identifying local needs, ensuring a coherent response and providing feedback to the departments of the city council. Headteachers in particular are seen as having a key role in developments and in responding to needs, especially of children and young people from ethnic minority backgrounds. They are regarded as part of the management structure of education services in the local authority. There is considerable face-to face contact with community groups and associations. The city has set up, through a democratic election process, a Migrants Council.

The City of Odense has established a structure of city services and committees which reflect a commitment to and understanding of the multi-level approach. It was put in place with the aim of improving services for all children, young people and adults, not specifically in relation to the needs of ethnic minority groups.

The processes of multi-level working experienced by staff within the city departments and schools in Odense reveal the following issues:

- clear explanations of the rationale for the restructuring of services are necessary and need to be led by the most senior people in departments

- training is needed for all the groups involved (teachers, social workers, youth and community workers, leisure and recreation staff), both in understanding the aims and processes involved in multi-level working and in knowing about and understanding each other's roles and areas of expertise

- developing positive attitudes in staff to these different ways of working is neither easy nor quickly achieved; shifting attitudes through training takes time

- putting a structure such as this in place will not by itself produce the desired effects. It is the ways of working within the structure which bring about improvements but the structure itself signals how services can be improved.

What has been learned?

- Education of ethnic minority children has to be promoted and supported through a multi-level approach in cities.

- A multi-level organisation and structure of city/local authority services provides an important lead on the value of multi-level approaches at local level.

- Thinking globally but acting locally and targeting resources where they are most needed is an important feature of a multi-level approach.

- Training and opportunities for staff from different areas to train and work alongside each other is a valuable long-term process without which multi-level working cannot succeed.

Main Outcomes

- The most important benefits of operating in the ways described above have so far been as follows:

- There is great benefit for all in terms of working relationships and understanding of roles; above all there is better provision and attention to the needs of pupils as individuals.

- Everyone in the system has better opportunities to learn as part of a learning organisation.

- It is possible to develop more innovative and better solutions which really help children and their parents.

- Individual cases and problems can be addressed more quickly and with greater flexibility.

- Children and their parents realise that close co-operation exists between the different agencies and find it more difficult to play one off against the other.

- The new ways of working ensure that fewer children 'disappear' within the system and so fewer underachieve.

Implications for in-service training

- It is important to provide cross-disciplinary training courses and meetings where staff from different disciplines can learn more about each other's roles and be trained together in different ways of working.

- These programmes run at different levels – for people who are completely new to the approach, those who have worked in Odense for a short time and those who are more advanced in the methodologies and ways of thinking required. The courses are run on the basis of one day per week for 6-10 weeks.

What staff and others have said about the development work

'Conferences organised by the District Committee have a direct effect on interdisciplinary co-operation in the District.'

'We have been given inspiration for multi-agency meetings in schools.'

'Our expectations of each other create co-operation between us.'

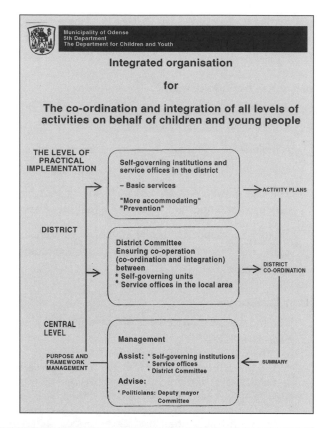

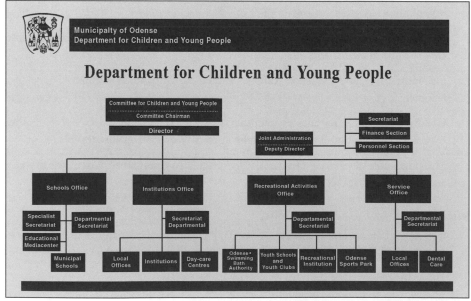

Case Study 2.5

Partner or Extended Schools (Brede School) Initiative, Rotterdam

Rotterdam; Paul Hoop
Tel: 31 10 2067112
Fax: 31 10 2067104
Email: p.hoop@dso.rotterdam.nl

Rotterdam has a significant and highly diverse ethnic minority population that amounts to over 50% of school pupils. It is not unusual for classes to have a large number of mother tongues represented. This and the fact that Rotterdam has a relatively young population overall poses a considerable challenge to the city authorities and to other organisations which support children. Rotterdam's educational policy is set in the broad context of an integrated youth policy.

Rotterdam has developed an integrated youth policy which covers a number of areas of development for young people, including education. Within the education section of the policy is the concept of 'Brede School'. The principles underpinning the Brede School concept are consistent with those which support the broader urban youth policy. After a significant number of primary and secondary schools had piloted the Brede School approach, all schools in Rotterdam are being encouraged to do so, through the policy of the city council and with the support of the other school boards.

These schools are the hub of education in their local community for the whole community – pupils, their parents and other adults. The activities extend well beyond the school day and cover holiday periods. They aim to improve children's achievement levels, encourage them to make active and positive use of their leisure time and to enhance parents' support for their education while improving their and other adults' own employment chances.

The schools attract resources from different sources and develop partnerships with other providers of educational opportunities, parents, local municipal authorities, social services and other organisations which support young people and scaffold their education, learning and personal development at school, at home and in their leisure time.

The Brede School Initiative

- is an integral part of integrated youth policy in Rotterdam – it sees multi-level working as a principle which underpins all education activity

- has a policy of opening schools up to the community and making them a hub of educational opportunities

- makes the best possible use of the resources provided by schools in terms of space, equipment and learning materials

- has a policy of ensuring equality of opportunity for all young people through the education system.

The basic principles of the Brede School concept are

- effective education in an affective school climate. This means paying great attention to the socio-emotional development of children and their personal and social skills

- forming productive links between the three contexts in which children and young people operate: home, school and their community or leisure time

- recognising that the school cannot achieve this alone and needs to seek partners with whom it can work

- using the full capacities and capabilities of the children, teachers, parents and organisations involved.

This development is characterised by:

- multi-level mainstream activity in Rotterdam in which all schools are now a part; what started as a project has now been embedded as an integral part of policy and practice for schools in the city

- educational activities which involve children, young people, parents, and other adults

- there are implications for all levels and many services and agencies within which the city services and agencies have to work in a multi-level way

- in the schools, the fundamental principle seems to be that headteachers have to provide considerable leadership and ensure that the developments are effectively managed

- treating all the people involved in or around the school on an equal footing.

What has been learned?

- schools which operate like this tend to produce better outcomes in terms of the achievement levels of their pupils, their personal and social development and attendance

- there is greater engagement of parents and other adults with the school and with the education of the young people

- the community around the school values the school highly and this positively affects the whole local community

- working like this has a particularly positive effect on many pupils from ethnic minority backgrounds, but there are significant issues to be overcome in terms of the engagement of their parents with activities at the school. Cultural mediation work is essential to this process and needs to involve people from the communities themselves

- schools cannot undertake all this work themselves – their main responsibility has to be to provide a high quality education within the school during the normal school day; a 'good school' is virtually a prerequisite for becoming a 'Brede School'

- building partnerships and involving a range of people and organisations is complex and time-consuming. Schools, and especially their headteachers, need support in doing and it makes sense, especially in areas served by several schools, to have an overall co-ordination facility provided through the partnerships which support the schools.

Main outcomes

- most partner schools report improved pupil achievement outcomes compared with before they became a partner school

- there have been positive effects on attendance, punctuality, achievement, attitude to school and education – and this also applies to parents' attitudes

- there are positive effects on the communities the schools serve in terms of education, employability and actual employment, social cohesion and welfare and reductions in youth crime, vandalism and other anti-social behaviour.

Case Study 2.6

The role of SUMES in multi-level working in Sheffield

Sheffield Education Department, SUMES (Sheffield Unified Multicultural Education Service): Zahid Hamid
Tel: ** 44 114 273 5703
Fax: ** 44 144 273 6279

(Also relevant to Theme D: Engaging Parents as Prime Educators of their Children)

Sheffield is a medium-sized city with a significant ethnic minority population, arriving from the 1950s onwards as industrial workers. Now large numbers are unemployed and are disadvantaged by low educational achievement and skill levels.

SUMES is the Education Department's service supporting black pupils, students and communities. It was developed in response to black people's complaints that the educational system was neglecting their languages, culture and experiences and so undermining the performance of ethnic minority pupils. SUMES is involved in strategic planning in the Education Department and with partnerships across the city with ethnic minority communities, parents, schools, local community organisations and other public and voluntary services.

Aims of SUMES

- to provide direct learning to black and bilingual pupils and students

- to develop new ideas and ways of working which will improve educational access and standards for black people

- to listen and consult closely with black parents and communities, identify and respond to needs by targeting resources, including staff, as appropriate

- to develop new and more relevant services for Sheffield's black communities.

This development is characterised by:
- a structure providing direct support to ethnic minority pupils and communities through eleven specialised projects

- multi-level working at all levels from individual pupils to whole city and national strategies

- the direction, policy and shape of the service is managed by the Local Authority in partnership with the ethnic minority communities through the SUMES Board, which is composed of representatives of these communities and of the Local Authority

- 90% of the SUMES staff are from the local ethnic minority communities, ensuring an organic link to these groups in the city

- professional staff from ethnic minority backgrounds manage the service on behalf of the City Council and the local communities.

What has been learned?
- People from ethnic minority communities must be involved in identifying and solving problems and responding to the needs that they have.

- It is necessary to work with the local ethnic minority communities at all stages of the process of identifying and responding to needs.

- By doing this, the Education Service has been able to highlight city-wide educational needs, work out specific strategies to meet them, deploy resources effectively and intelligently and plan future development and local community participation.

- A fundamental element of this approach is to recognise, value and utilise the diverse resources of the ethnic minority communities themselves, both in planning and working through solutions and in staffing the service.

Some outcomes
To provide illustrations of what can be achieved, listed below in summary are the achievements for 1996/97 of just three of the SUMES projects (*more information can be obtained from SUMES through the contact numbers provided*).

Activities and Structure of SUMES

Structure

SUMES has an area-based structure. The areas relect school clusters. Each area has a Head and a Deputy. The Area Managers have responsibility for particular aspects of city-wide work

Area 1: South Sheffield

Area 2: North and East Sheffield
(Clusters A, B and H-part)
Community Liaison

Area 3: Central and West Sheffield
Training

Services for Schools and Communities

• English as a second language
bilingual teachers support individuals and classes to allow full access to the curriculum

• African-Caribbean Support
Curriculum, pastoral and cultural support for African-Caribbean pupils

• Under Five's
individual families and schools are supported through nursery-based child care assistants and home tutors

• Community Liaison
Home visiting and the development of links between schools, parents and the community

• Special Needs
Child care assistants and teachers work with children with special needs in mainstream and special schools

• Reading Projects
SUMES has a Reading Task Force with reading recovery teachers and reading assistants to improve literacy levels in primary schools

• Education Social Work
Specialist staff work with communities on issues such as non-attendance at school. They advise on Child Protection issues

Central Services

Expertise, advice and support on race and cultural issues in education

• Training support for SUMES staff and for schools and support services

• Multicultural library

• Publications
Leaflets and booklets on SUMES services and educational issues including a termly newsletter and a Languages Survey published every two years

• Development work
SUMES continually seeks to develop new and effective services, often in partnership with other agencies or community groups. Multi-lingual City, an initiative to raise the profile of languages in the city, is one example

(a) SUMES Under 5s Project: 22 staff

The project aims for a smooth transition from home into nursery school, raising levels of acquisition of English, increasing access to the curriculum and improving parental involvement and community links. 415 new children were settled into nurseries within three months because of the involvement of black and bilingual staff; 358 children received pre-admission visits as part of their induction into Nursery; 477 parents were involved in the transitional work from home to Nursery; 477 children made significant progress in acquiring a basic level of English whilst another 487 children made measurable progress at higher levels.

(b) African-Caribbean Curriculum and Pastoral Development Service: Secondary Education: 5 staff

This project aims to improve the command of language appropriate for learning, to strengthen partnerships between home and school, to improve curriculum access and the opportunities to achieve at higher levels, especially in the 'core' subjects of English, mathematics and science, to improve careers advice and guidance and support for pupils' welfare in the school, to remove cultural and racist barriers to equality of opportunity in education and reduce confrontational situations in and out of class. The project also aims to reduce the present disproportionate exclusion of African and Caribbean pupils from schools.

280 pupils showed an improvement in the core subjects; 336 pupils showed increased motivation in subjects which had some cultural relevance to African and Caribbean as well as Asian and European people; 201 pupils in eight schools have been taught to use standard English without Creole vocabulary and structures in curriculum work and 405 pupils received direct in-class support which improved their motivation and/or achievement.

451 pupils and parents were given counselling and advice and 326 homes were visited to improve home/school liaison covering pupils from ten schools. 97 pupils were given transition support to help them settle down in their new schools.

(c) Special Educational Needs of Black Pupils: 9 Staff

This project assesses the special educational needs experienced by black pupils; supports pupils with learning difficulties by using a variety of materials and methodologies designed to maximise progress; monitors progress and evaluates strategies to ensure that education is enhanced for black and bilingual pupils with identified difficulties related to achievement; involves the parents of pupils experiencing learning difficulties and contacts support agencies when appropriate. 67 black pupils experiencing special educational needs were assessed and the progress of 54 was monitored; 70 parents were encouraged to participate in providing support for their children's learning.

92 hearing-impaired pupils were supported by a bilingual support initiative, and 39 were assessed to identify their special needs. 91 pupils were supported in curriculum activities and and the Education Psychology Service was involved in advising 53 parents on the education of their children.

Implications for in-service training

Staff from ethnic minority backgrounds need to be involved in professional development. SUMES set up a programme to enable staff to acquire further qualifications. 10% of staff time was set aside for in-service training, to develop their professional skills and knowledge, share experience and practice, take part in curriculum development activities and develop their own practice.

- a two year primary-based teaching qualification (B.Ed.) was established in 1991 in Language Studies at Sheffield Hallam University. 40 SUMES staff gained qualified teacher status through this route – a major and crucial investment in the skills of black and bilingual staff

- SUMES has also developed an accredited initial training course targeted at the needs of new SUMES Support Teachers. Access to Bilingual Support Workers Training is a one-year programme of which the transmission of practical teaching skills and knowledge forms a strong element

- black and bilingual staff can make a major contribution to race equality training of the wider staff of an education service, including teachers in schools.

What one child said...

It was great that the school had an Asian teacher who could understand and relate to me. My mum wasn't fluent in English and at that time I needed support in learning to speak, read and write in English.

Farhat Rafiq was a bright girl at a Sheffield school who was identified by the school's SUMES support teacher as needing support in subjects like mathematics and science. She is now studying four A-Levels but still goes back to her primary school every Tuesday morning to help give young Asian children the same kind of support she received during her early years at school. She says 'If it wasn't for SUMES, people like me would not be where we are now. SUMES recognised the skills I had and put them to good effect. I am grateful for that. I have gained so much in the last ten years'.

Case Study 2.7

City leadership on multi-level working in Turin

City of Turin, Luca Palese
Tel: ** 39 011 442 9130
Fax: ** 39 011 442 9126
E-Mail: centridoc@comune.torino.it

The City of Turin does not have responsibility for the statutory school system; in common with the rest of Italy, schools are responsible to the Education Ministry through the Provincial Education Office (*Provedditorato*). The City makes or co-ordinates educational provision for pre-school and nursery, adult education and a range of additional educational opportunities as indicated in Theme E.

The City is involved in a number of educational networks including DIECEC and the Educating Cities network. This, and the high level of investment in non-statutory education, illustrate the great importance which the city attaches to investment in the education of its citizens, including its growing ethnic minority population.

Education in the city is the responsibility at political level of a deputy mayor (*Assessore*) who has a deep commitment to the value of diversity and to the multi-level approach. The visits of the DIECEC co-ordinator to Turin revealed a high level of understanding of the principles and practices which underpin the Network, and a considerable commitment to implementing them.

The *assessore* for Education in Turin believes that co-ordination of services and co-operation between them have to function well in a system where responsibility for education lies with different organisations. Notwithstanding the apportioning of responsibilities for education, there is a clear understanding of multi-level working and the need to scaffold children's and young people's education at home and in the community as well as at school. The importance of intercultural education is also fully appreciated.

These convictions are demonstrated in a number of ways:

- for the past four years, Turin has placed a major focus on the value of diversity and the need for social integration. This has been achieved through high profile events, good publicity and high level political representation of these themes

- there is a level of co-operation between the Provincial Education Office, The Region and the City at senior levels

- Turin works closely with a wide range of services and organisations to seek to provide a good support system for education outside school

- considerable additional support in the form of funding for children from ethnic minority backgrounds and for those with special educational needs

- the city has established an Intercultural Centre (see Theme F)

Some of the Aims of City Education Leadership and Policy

- to ensure a good level of co-operation between different services and organisations responsible for educational services

- to ensure coherence of provision between non-statutory and statutory education, for example in the provision of pre-school and nursery classes

- to provide additional resources to respond to the needs of educationally disadvantaged groups, including ethnic minority children and young people

- to put in place a comprehensive and co-ordinated programme of educational activities which enhance the curriculum of schools and provide wide-ranging opportunities for children, young people and adults to learn

- to promote the value of diversity and the important contribution of education to social integration and harmony and to economic prosperity and the quality of life of Turin's citizens.

This development is characterised by:

- a major commitment in terms of political leadership, backed up by resources, to promoting education and the value of diversity in a city

- personal leadership on difficult issues is vital to the promotion of policies in favour of ethnic minority children and their families

- a clear understanding of the principles and practices which underpin multi-level working

- a determination to see issues affecting ethnic minority children as part of a broader commitment to social justice and equality

- even in complex administration systems, clear leadership can produce policies and practices which provide important support co-ordinated with provision made by other administrative authorities

- it is possible to establish good links between statutory and non-statutory educational provision and to ensure that ethnic minority children are able to access the additional support they need to help them to achieve.

Case Study 2.8

The Cork Education Centre: Supporting multi-level approaches to education through in-service training and curriculum/educational project development

Cork Education Centre
Bart Bambury, Director
Tel: ** 353 21 501115
Fax:** 353 21 501161
E-Mail: ioc@tinet.ie

The Cork Education System is part of a network of Education Centres established across Ireland. They have responsibility for organising and providing in-service training and curriculum development work in support of national developments and in response to the needs of local teachers and people involved in the education of children and young people. The Centres have a basic level of staffing, consisting of a Centre Director and an Administrator. They build up local networks and the trainers for in-service pro-grammes are drawn from local, regional and national sources and include many practis-ing teachers. The Cork Education Centre is the hub of DIECEC's operation in Cork and the involvement of many schools and people in DIECEC projects is organised through the Centre.

The Cork Education Centre changed its name from 'Cork Teachers Centre' to reflect its multi-level approach to education and training. It is involved with parents' organisa-tions, other local providers of education such as University College, the Cork City Corporation, the Traveller Education programme and many other local partners. It illustrates how strong local networks can be promoted, established and built up as an infrastructure for enabling multi-level approaches to be developed.

Aims of the Centre

- to promote and provide an integrated, partnership approach to education in Cork

- to provide for and promote the professional development of teachers and other people involved in education and training

- to network good practice and promote improvements in the curriculum in schools

- to promote the notions of multi-level working, including the role of parents as prime educators of their children, through its approach to developments in Cork and the specific involvement of people and institutions in DIECEC projects

The Centre has a Management Committee mainly consisting of teachers, including some principals. There is appropriate representation of different phases and sectors. The Centre Director is responsible to the Management Committee, which also helps to prioritise, organise and promote professional development activities. The Centre Direc-tor networks actively with a wide range of partners in educational processes and institutions in Cork, through a personal approach which illustrates a commitment to multi-level working, and to promoting and disseminating good practice.

Many in-career programmes are initiated by the Centre in response to local teacher/school needs. Teachers are given major roles in the creation, delivery and evaluation of programmes. Teacher interest support groups working with and through the centre also respond to locally identified needs. The Centre, working in collaboration with the Department of Education and Science in Dublin, organises and administers in-service courses in the context of national programmes and developments, for example in the uses of information and communications technology. It has a multi-media library.

A high level of ownership and responsibility is vested in the people. The principals (headteachers) of schools are involved with particular priority in the organisation and delivery of in-service programmes. The open door, neutral status of the Centre creates opportunities to develop partnerships and challenge traditional thinking and approaches. It has created links and working relationships with all the educational agencies in the city and plays a key role as a regional dissemination and information centre.

What has been learned?

- a wide range of partners need to be involved in any successful educational development

- well-targeted, good quality professional development is a key component of multi-level approaches

- networking and the development of productive partnerships with a wide range of agencies and services is an essential element of any education system. Because all systems involve a wide range of organisations, links need to be forged between them. An organisation or institution has to take the lead in this

- multi-level working is not easy. Despite the best efforts to include all appropriate partners, some people can be left out; those who are involved may find it difficult to sustain a collaborative approach. Multi-level working itself has to be well supported

- an organisation, centre or agency which has a neutral or indirect role in terms of its responsibility for the direct delivery of educational services to children and young people is well placed to develop and maintain partnerships with organisations which do.

Main outcomes

- the Centre's partnership/multi-level approach has impacted at many levels within Cork's educational community over the past twenty years. All Centre activities are seen as opportunities to involve 'other players'

- in-career training programmes are designed and provided in collaboration with other relevant agencies wherever possible. For example, they involve the Business Community, Arts Organisations, Parents, the Health Board)

- The creation of such partnerships has resulted not only in better courses but also in further developmental work which brings together teachers and other people from schools and from the other organisations, with mutual benefits. Teachers have good opportunities for further learning and the activities result in a greater reaching out by schools into the wider community

- Involvement in a wide range of European projects has created learning opportunities and leadership roles for teachers. Teachers involved in these programmes share their experiences with other colleagues at in-service sessions and often assist with the process of challenging existing or traditional approaches and methodologies. Wherever possible, Department of Education and Science Inspectors, parents and management representatives of relevant educational agencies are involved. Involvement in European projects has helped to create a particular focus in schools on intercultural policies and practices.

- the Centre's work has a particular focus on disadvantaged and marginalised children and young people and prioritises the work of schools and teachers in their support.

- the Centre promotes and supports opportunities to display children's work to the public.

- Parents are very much involved in the work of the Centre, especially through the productive links with parents' organisations and associations. The Centre supports programmes which involve parents and parents learning alongside teachers.

Implications for In-Service Training

In-service training and other forms of professional development are essential to the development of multi-level working. Training in/exemplification of the success of the approach is a starting point; involvement in transnational projects is a way of developing awareness, knowledge, skills and understanding of multi-level approaches.

Teachers need confidence and support in working in new ways, especially those which open up schools to parents and to the community. They also need training and support in examining their own professional practice (for example, through action research) with regard to multi-level working.

Training is required at initial and in-service stages in the multi-level approach. but as yet does not figure to any great extent. This key to more successful working with diverse pupil populations and in schools in disadvantaged areas needs to be provided at an early stage in teachers' and others' professional training and development.

SECTION THREE
MULTI-LEVEL WORKING IN SCHOOLS

Over 40 people work regularly in this school; only 12 of us are teachers. Some people are volunteers. We all contribute to the education of the children and many of us to learning in the whole community. But everything we do is designed to improve the children's education. We educate the children at the times when the parents are not there to do this themselves.

These are the words of the headteacher of a school which seeks to be the hub of education in its community and which illustrates the concept of the multi-level school.

A multi-level school understands that children's and young people's education requires effective scaffolding not just at school, but at home and in their community. As a result, the school takes steps, not by itself but working in partnerships with its parents, pupils and community. It designs educational developments that positively affect pupils, teachers, other school staff, parents and the wider community. It also works closely with other professional services from the public, private and voluntary sectors, and with the authorities who have responsibility for it, to put this scaffolding in place. The school sees this as an essential part of raising the achievement levels and improving the life chances of its pupils, their parents and the community it serves. A basic pre-requisite for developing this approach is that the schools itself provides a high quality education.

The characteristics of multi-level schools

Multi-level schools have all or most of the following characteristics:

- a shared understanding among the people who work in and with them that children and young people from ethnic minority backgrounds need strong support for their education from three sources: school, home and their community

- a system of values which recognises and regards equally the contribution of everyone who works with the children and their families, and holds the children and families themselves in high regard

- recognition that education and learning should start from well before children attend the school and continue throughout life: a commitment to life-long learning

- regular and positive contact with parents and guardians, including many and meaningful opportunities for discussion of their children's progress

- recognition that the school has a duty to be open to parents, to work with them as equal partners and to acknowledge and use for the pupils' benefit the skills, knowledge and understanding parents can provide, as well as working with them so they can effectively support their children's education

- provision, through partnership with other organisations, of a wide range of educational opportunities during and after school and in school holidays, and a recognition that many adults other than qualified teachers can make important contributions

- strong and effective policies and practice for the rapid development of pupils' home and second or additional languages

- arrangements, for example class and school councils, by which pupils are listened to and their views taken into account about aspects of their education and lives

- determination that children and young people of whatever background will achieve at high levels and develop an increasing responsibility for their own learning. A positive view of the potential of all pupils to achieve at high levels whatever their background is central

- recognition that the school needs to respond to the specific cultural, faith and linguistic backgrounds and overall educational needs of its pupils

- school doors which, as a result of co-operation with others, are open from early in the morning to late in the evening, most days of the year

- a climate which encourages, recognises and rewards success at the level of the individual pupil and values their contribution to the school

- good systems for monitoring and supporting the progress of individual pupils, identifying strengths and weaknesses and building on or addressing them at an early stage.

Good multi-level schools have all the characteristics associated with good schools generally. For example, they have highly effective leadership and management, quality teaching, well-motivated staff, effective processes for staff development, well-deployed resources, well-developed systems of monitoring and support for individual pupils, effective internal processes for evaluation and planning and high expectations of their pupils. DIECEC's experience of multi-level schools suggests that the qualities of leadership and management provided by the headteacher are crucial.

Although the above might suggest a huge increase in workload, the evidence indicates otherwise. Partnerships with others are vital – no school can fulfil the criteria set out above from its own human and other resources – but so is the reality that a multi-level approach helps to convert problems into solutions and reduces the levels of disruption and 'hassle'. Rather than more work, it produces different work; it also, potentially and in practice, harnesses much support for the school.

Levels of Achievement

Good multi-level schools have clear proof that their pupils achieve at increasingly higher levels and that the school is having a positive effect on the quality of life in its communities. There is a clear difference between the concept of the 'multi-level' school' and that of the 'community school': multi-level schools focus all of their activities in some way or other on the achievement levels of their pupils – they help parents and other adults to achieve as well, but only in ways which are helpful to the pupils. This is not to say that community schools do not or cannot operate in this way, only to clarify the concept of the multi-level school. The schools included in the case studies can demonstrate considerable improvements in their pupils' levels of achievement as a result of adopting a multi-level approach.

DIECEC's experience has been that multi-level schools work especially well for pupils from ethnic minority backgrounds and for pupils with a high level of educational disadvantage. Under-performing schools in advantaged areas can reap significant benefits from this approach.

The Triangle of Home, School and Community

We have emphasised that multi-level working involves the scaffolding of pupils' education at home, in the community and at school. Multi-level schools place their pupils in the centre of this triangle:

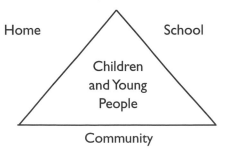

Home School

Children
and Young
People

Community

This triangle functions optimally when all three vertices are working well and harmoniously. It may even work quite well when two of the vertices are operating effectively – especially home and school. The triangle has to be a dynamic entity; multi-level schools see themselves as the hub which enables the triangle to function, as well as being one of its vertices.

Why 'the hub'?

A hub enables a wheel to function; if it is driven or controlled, then this is usually by other mechanisms. DIECEC represents multi-level schools as hubs of education in their community because it sees in practice that schools which cater effectively for diversity seek not to control other educational provision in the community but to promote, facilitate, co-ordinate and influence it.

The issue of 'control' as opposed to 'leadership and empowerment' is crucial to the concept of multi-level working in and around schools. Schools which cater well for diverse populations have to respond to the differing backgrounds of their pupils, and to their individual needs. This is important for any school, but especially so where there are different cultural, faith and linguistic heritages.

Schools which respond well to cultural diversity have to be flexible; their population may change rapidly (for example, as the result of an influx of refugee children); the needs of the children or young people may be very different from one year to the next. The characteristics of the curriculum and management of such schools are discussed in more detail later in this section. Schools which seek to control education in their community through the curriculum of the school and other measures, and to impose a culture on their pupils which may be at odds with culture of home and the community, are much less likely to be successful than those which make a flexible response.

This means welcoming the diversity of the pupils and their backgrounds and responding to them in such a way that pupils want to learn and are able to learn, supported by their parents or guardians and the community. It does not mean a lowering of standards, accepting second best, making excuses for the children or tolerating the unacceptable in terms of behaviour, quality and quantity of work or normal human and social values. There is absolutely no contradiction between multi-level schools which make a flexible response to diversity, and high levels of achievement. In fact the reverse is the case: in DIECEC's experience, these schools are much more likely to enable their pupils to achieve at higher levels.

Implementing the multi-level approach in individual schools

For every city and every education system there will be parameters within which additional provision in and around the school must take place. These include legal and safety requirements, child protection, assurances of quality etc. Schools must find the appropriate balance between these parameters and empowering people from the local community to both provide and access learning opportunities. Too much emphasis on the mandatory requirements will drive potential partners away; insufficient emphasis can lead to severe problems.

This does not mean that potential providers of opportunities for learning will form an orderly queue at the school, offering their services. The school must, through its own staff or people from local communities (cultural mediators who can form productive bridges between these communities and the school) or both, go out to the community and persuade people to participate. There are a variety of mechanisms for doing this, and a combination of the following is probably the most effective way forward:

- headteachers should make an important contribution, by giving a professional lead, co-ordinating overall strategy and actively promoting the school and its philosophy within the community. Governors or managers can promote the approach and bring in people from the local and wider community

- parents who come into school can be powerful advocates for the school and its desire to promote a whole community approach; they, and other parents, should be key players in any strategy

- staff with a particular role in home/school liaison or cultural mediation should play a major role – whether or not they work in the school or Education Service

- teachers and school staff, especially teaching and non-teaching staff who live in the local community, can contribute considerably to the strategy and its implementation. But this role should not extend to the point where it deflects teaching staff from their prime role of providing a high quality education for the pupils

- pupils and students can play an important role, especially alongside their parents

- professional staff from other services (public, private and voluntary) can help the school to promote its message.

It has been found useful to set up a community committee or management group which takes responsibility for this aspect of the school's activities. In some cases community trusts or other bodies have been set up, either in relation to an individual school or to co-ordinate additional educational opportunities across a community served by a number of schools (see below).

Implementing the multi-level approach in schools which serve an area or community

The model outlined is effective for a single school in an area or the only one prepared to operate in a multi-level way. Another model suits communities where a number of schools are catering for a particular area – as in densely populated urban areas and especially where there is high ethnic minority settlement.

This model involves partnerships between schools, referred to as 'families', 'clusters' or 'associations', or community partnerships which work with all the schools in the area. Essentially, the schools co-operate over the co-ordination of additional activities, with the support of their city and/or local authority. Cities fulfilling the role they have developed as members of DIECEC will increasingly see this as their responsibility; they will promote this collaborative approach between schools, assure co-ordination and provide other practical support. More details of the cities' role in this are set out in Section Two.

Some of the reasons for using this co-operative model are as follows:

- it corresponds to the notion of multi-level and multi-agency working: if other organisations are to work with schools, then schools should work together for the benefit of their community, even where there is some competition between them

- it ensures a coherent approach to opportunities for learning in the community. For example, it is possible to ensure that there is a response to identified learning needs, to eliminate duplication and fill gaps

- it can ensure a more comprehensive programme as a result

- it makes better use of resources and provides better value for money

- it means that other organisations can make a coherent response based on all the schools in the community, rather than a fragmented one, and that the need for this approach is better appreciated by the whole service or organisation.

If a number of schools are involved, a co-ordinator may be needed to liase between the schools and other providers of learning opportunities, make links with parents and ensure that local people know about and can access the provision. The co-ordination work can be done more cost- and time-effectively when it is in one person's hands.

Setting up a Community Committee to oversee this work can be a useful mechanism; this group might have a wider remit (for example, bidding for additional resources for the area, attracting or raising funds to support a wider range of educational opportunities). Its membership will depend on local circumstances, but it should be based solidly in the community itself.

Cities (or education authorities if these are different bodies) and schools should co-operate over this issue and ensure coherent provision prioritising areas of multiple disadvantage. 'Learning Cities' will promote this model and engage schools actively in participation in multi-level working as a main plank of their strategy for school improvement and particularly raising pupils' achievement.

There is evidence that where this happens, the benefits are not about education alone. There are important broader effects in terms of the sustainability of communities, social harmony and welfare and, in the longer term, economic prosperity, adding up to a better quality of life for people in these communities. The number of potential and actual providers of good learning opportunities for children and young people also increases, beginning an upward spiral of achievement.

The extent of the role and responsibility of schools in implementing a multi-level approach

Schools have people who are trained to ensure good teaching and effective learning, and specific resources to support their work. They are often situated in the centre of a community (but see the note below about situations where they are not!) so are well placed to provide and co-ordinate educational opportunities. A key message of this Handbook is that schools must involve outsiders if they are to be real learning centres for their communities. Why? Because.....

- teachers and schools cannot do it alone. Teachers will find the workload impossible to sustain and may end up trying to do work for which they are not trained. Neither is it reasonable to expect teachers to work the hours demanded by the multi-level model

- teachers need to be able to concentrate on their core task: teaching and helping children and young people to learn. While other people can contribute to these processes during school time and teachers can contribute to other activities, their main professional responsibility is to plan, implement and evaluate teaching and learning. To do so effectively requires time well beyond the school day

- teachers and others working in schools need to feel that children's learning and education are being well supported outside school. At the same time, they have to accept (and welcome!) the idea that many other people can make a positive contribution to pupils' learning and development. Where teachers feel that their pupils' progress is well-scaffolded outside school hours, there is evidence that their morale is raised

- many adults other than teachers, be they professionals or volunteers (the latter with some training), and especially parents, have skills, experience and knowledge which can make an important contribution to pupils' learning and to their view of the importance of education. Many of them are willing to share these with children and young people, in and outside school

- a wide range of people from different backgrounds and with different experiences will influence children and young people in their lives outside school, and preparation for this is an important part of learning

- different cultures and religious traditions take different approaches to learning and the schools need to reflect these in their work with pupils. People from non-dominant cultures or faiths can indicate similarities with other cultures and faiths of the country and city

- many professional adults have skills and knowledge which teachers lack. Although many teachers rightly want to be 'multi-skilled' (for example, by developing counselling skills), their main professional responsibility is to continue to develop as teachers and providers of opportunities for learning, and to ensure that children and young people achieve as highly as they can. Teachers should not be asked to undertake work outside of their professional remit; equally, other professionals with highly-developed skills should not be obliged to correct mistakes made by others

- marginalised people often require specific help and support and from a specific source. Working with the parents of children who have greatest difficulty in learning at school may be most effective if it is done through other members of the same community

Schools serving a dispersed pupil population

In cities with numerous areas of educational disadvantage, or where a predominant community is dispersed across several schools, a multi-level approach presents practical problems especially in engaging parents. More work is needed on this but DIECEC has established that the multi-level approach needs to be co-ordinated by the city across all areas. This enables the direct engagement of parents in learning activities which enable them to support their children's education. Although ICT offers potential solutions, project work in this area tends to gloss over the practicalities and costs of access for both schools and families. Ultimately the schools which serve dispersed populations need a co-ordinated city-wide multi-level approach most of all. Taking the view that any system is only as good as its effectiveness in the toughest circumstances, the difficulties facing these schools ought to serve as criteria for a city's or whole education system's support for multi-level working.

A pivotal role for schools

Although schools should not and cannot implement the multi-level approach by themselves, they must assume the pivotal role. Their position within communities, their resources, expertise and availability ought to mean that they are, or are becoming, the hub of education and learning in their community. They should be reaching out to parents and other adults and engaging them in additional opportunities for learning, both as providers and participants, whether in the school or elsewhere at other times. But their first emphasis is on providing excellent education, while also supporting parents and promoting and helping implement multi-level working and 'whole community education' with their pupils, parents and the wider community.

Implications for school management

High quality leadership and management are clearly critical factors in raising the achievement levels of pupils. Headteachers need to develop and project a vision of education in their community which transcends the basic requirement of assuring the quality of education within the formal curriculum. If they do not lead strongly on this issue, little is likely to change in terms of the achievement levels of ethnic minority children and young people. Their education will often be unsupported outside school and underachievement will remain likely even in schools which provide a 'good' basic education. This can leave teachers with the frustrating feeling that they are getting nowhere.

Headteachers have the right to expect philosophical, pedagogical and practical support from their city and local, regional or national education authority. Cities cannot expect headteachers to pick up this baton if they do not themselves project the importance of lifelong learning and a multi-level approach which scaffolds education at home, in the community and at school. Authorities with responsibility for education cannot expect headteachers to promote or develop this vision by themselves.

A comprehensive in-service training programme is needed for headteachers and other senior staff (especially aspiring headteachers) which includes the 'normal' competences associated with headship but extends also to the philosophy and practical skills associated with the multi-level approach: intercultural skills; understanding of the cultural, linguistic and faith backgrounds of the communities; how to interact successfully with parents and the community as well as with the pupils. Recruitment of staff from the same backgrounds as the children is an issue. It may be possible in schools which serve a bi-or tri-cultural population, but not always in a school which serves pupils from a wide range of heritages.

Examples of appropriate training and development programmes exist in the DIECEC cities. Sometimes the headteachers have developed their own programmes in collaboration with a teacher training institution – often their local university – and their education authority. National programmes rarely take serious account of the needs of diverse populations. A comprehensive, accredited training programme should be available to all teachers and school staff.

Schools have to focus on their core business of providing quality education for all their pupils but how to achieve it requires special consideration in light of the multi-level approach. The headteacher and staff of schools which serve ethnic minority pupils must have a vision of education and learning which fits the multi-level approach. It is for headteachers to promote the approach, co-ordinating its implementation and reflecting it in their leadership and management.

This means, for example, considering the multi-level implications of the whole-school processes of curriculum planning, implementation, review and evaluation. When a multi-level school identifies literacy as a major focus for development work, it will consider this with its partners (including parents, the wider community and other organisations and services) and design a strategy which reflects a whole community approach to improving literacy. This is both so that parents and others in the community improve their own levels of literacy and (most importantly) so that pupils' work at school is reinforced by what is happening at home and in the wider community. The characteristics of the multi-level school must be promoted consistently and coherently with the rest of the staff and multi-level working must be exemplified in the management processes in the school. As one headteacher observed.

> You cannot just operate in a multi-level way when working at school with parents or other organisations; the approach has to be reflected in how you work with your colleagues, and you have to 'live' the approach yourself. It's not just something you do when you arrive at school in the morning – it's really a way of life.

Case Study 3.1

Working with parents and the community to raise achievement at Birchfield Primary School, Birmingham

Name of School: Birchfield Community Primary School, Birmingham
Headteacher: Andrew Saunders
Contact telephone/fax/email:
Tel: 00 44 121 554 0661
Fax: 00 44 121 551 0231

Birchfield Community Primary School is in Aston, an inner-city area of Birmingham. It serves 640 children and their families plus 120 children who attend a pre-school play-group and nursery unit. The community originates predominantly from Pakistan, Bangladesh and India. There is a strong partnership between school, parents and the wider community, with a range of activities based in a community house (Trinity House) and a Home/School Partnership Team which undertakes home visits and promotes the school's 'open door' policy.

Birchfield is constantly seeking to raise its achievement levels and has developed a framework within which these levels can and do rise. Pupils now achieve at or above national expectations. Elements of this framework include:

* defined curriculum plans which ensure that all pupils access the National Curriculum

* monitoring and evaluation of pupils' progress and also the performance of teachers

* stated school policies in which parents have been involved and which they understand

* commitment to the professional development of staff in partnership with the University of Central England

* a School Council which involves children in taking responsibility and making decisions, to support good behaviour and develop pupils' self-esteem.

Aims of the multi-level work

* to raise standards across the school

* to create a strong partnership with parents and the wider community

* to help parents to support their children's education at home, and to work with the school

* to raise levels of education and training in the community so as to improve its sustainability and capacity for self-improvement

* to raise the esteem of parents in the eyes of their children through recognising their achievements.

There are regular parents' evenings and parents are welcome to visit the school at any time. Specific activities for parents include:

- curriculum afternoons in which staff curriculum specialists explain and advise about mathematics, English, history, etc. Parents can see children working and participate in tasks alongside the children

- year group meetings at which the parents meet class teachers and discuss in detail the programme of study for a particular year so they can give greater support at home

- the Home/School Partnership Team are available to meet individual parents at home or school to discuss any concerns they have and to follow up concerns expressed by teachers.

The school has a converted house on its site which is home to a pre-school playgroup and provides a community room where parents can get school information. There are six rooms for adult and community classes, a toy library and community kitchen. A range of classes is on offer at the house, including literacy, numeracy, Urdu, English for speakers of other languages and word-processing. The school organises community afternoons to tackle local concerns and raise the awareness of the community of services such as Health and Recreation. The school has co-ordinated and brought in these resources – financial, human and in the form of educational and recreational activities funded through other means. Although the school has the advantage of the community house, much of the work with parents and the basic philosophy of the school could be realised without this facility.

This development is characteristised by:

- a multi-level school approach, developed through the vision and activities of the school itself, with strong support from the governing body

- the engagement of parents in ways which have supported children's learning and educational progress in schools, at home and in their community

- the engagement of the wider community in the activities of the school and in their own learning and training to raise levels of employability and support for education in a deprived area

- strong out-reach support for parents and the community

- recognising and rewarding parents' as well as pupils' achievements

- raising children's awareness of ways their parents can help them with their learning

- levering in additional resources from a range of sources by the school, with many other people and agencies involved in the organization and delivery of activities

- strong and effective leadership of the work in the school and with parents and the community from the headteacher, other staff in the school and the governing body.

What has been learned?

- achievement levels rise quite significantly as a result of internal school improvement combined with close involvement of parents and the wider community in children's education

- parents are crucial in the education and learning of their children

- broader community support for and understanding of education can be accomplished by a dynamic partnership between home, school and the community

- time spent working with parents is an investment in the achievement levels of the children as opposed to a cost

- additional resources can be drawn in from a variety of sources, but this is time-consuming and requires a person or people to undertake the contact work and make arrangements

- any initiative in a school should be focused on the education of the children – all Birchfield's work aims to provide the highest possible standard of education and care for the children, in partnership with home, mutually raising standards and expectations.

Main outcomes:

- the achievement levels of children at the school have risen from a low level in 1992 to a point where they attain nationally expected levels for 7 *and* 11 years olds as measured by national assessments of English, mathematics and science – a notable achievement where many children start school with little or no English

- the educational levels of many parents have risen over the past five years to the point where they can access employment at higher levels. Some of the parents now undertake important work within the school

- the self-esteem and confidence of parents and pupils have risen considerably

- parents feel much more confident about their ability to support their children's education at school, and to help them through educational activities at home

- the community around the school has a higher level of education and employability

- the school is greatly over-subscribed and its standing and reputation in the community have been considerably enhanced.

Implications for in-service training:

- in-service programmes for headteachers, teachers, governors and educational administrators need to include a strong element related to the roles of parents and the wider community in raising achievement levels and improving mutual understanding between schools and their communities

- these programmes should include practical examples of ways in which schools and education systems have involved parents and the wider community in education and learning which both supports their children's learning and raises their own educational levels and self-esteem

- headteachers and governors need to work closely together on a strategy for multi-level working in their schools; they must beware the idea that they can undertake all of this through their own resources and engage the support and practical help of a range of others

- training in areas such as engaging parents, community development and capacity building and opening up schools to the community are specific elements which cities and education systems can provide to support schools in their efforts to develop a multi-level approach which suits their circumstances.

Case Study 3.2

Multi-level working in support of ethnic minority pupils at Roihuvoiri Primary School

Name of School: Roihuvoiri Primary School, Helsinki
Headteacher: Satu Honkala
Contact telephone/fax/email: satu.honkala@freenet.hut.fi
Riitta Veinio (Helsinki City Council Education Department)
Tel: ** 358 9 310 829 00
Fax: ** 358 9 310 829 04

Roihuvoiri Primary School is situated in the eastern part of Helsinki. 20% of the pupils and 15% of the staff of 35 have Finnish as a second language and sixteen languages other than Finnish are spoken as first languages in the school, with Russian, Estonian and Somalian the most common. Pupils total about 470. The school has preparatory classes/teaching groups for pupils whose first language is not Finnish and who need additional help with it.

The school is developing a non-graded, individualised learning system, meaning that children are not grouped according to their level. It normally takes Finnish pupils between 5 and 7 years to complete primary education. The school seeks to develop itself as a multicultural school. Acquiring thinking skills, taking responsibility and initiative and independent learning skills are important aims of the school. There is a major emphasis on enabling emergent bilingual pupils to become truly bilingual and to have a command of language required for successful study in upper level secondary school.

The school is part of a developing system of education in the area, from day care for infants through to upper level secondary education and beyond. There are further facilties for education in leisure time through youth work and a music school. The school is part of a national school improvement project. The five main themes at

Roihuvoiri are: non-graded education (individual curricula, non-competetitive assessment, different ages in the same teaching group), changes in the roles of staff coupled to in-service training, develping evaluation at pupil, teacher and whole school levels, a flexible school admission system (pupils can start between age 6 and 8 and at different times during the year) and specific attention to the needs of ethnic minority pupils.

The multi-level work embraces

- extensive work with parents to involve them in their children's education and provide them with knowledge and skills which wil help them

- multi-agency working, especially with social services and health care

- common activities and close co-operation with day care facilties for younger children and offering a range of after-school activities aimed at helping young ethnic minority children to integrate and to make good use of their time

- co-operation with pre-school classes and other schools (secondary) to create a continuous education plan for each ethnic minority child, from preschool to secondary school

- religious and cultural teaching provided by people from the local communities to support children's home culture and language

- co-operation with embassies and other education ministries to support home language and cultural development

- mother tongue teachers and majority language speakers acting as classroom assistants in school to help children and provide positive role models

- specific intercultural activities to create respect for other cultures, and a multi-cultural ethos in school

- co-operation with the local newspaper to present a positive image of diversity and help to combat racism.

This development is characterised by an approach to the education of ethnic minority pupils which places them at the centre of the school's main aims and development priorities and involves people from their communities – both professionals and volunteers. Attention is paid to their spiritual, social and cultural needs and to their learning of the Finnish language.

Case Study 3.3

Developing intercultural education and raising achievement at Panzini-Zappa Lower Secondary School, Bologna

Name of School: Panzini-Zappa Lower Secondary School, Bologna
Headteacher: Clara Dalle Vacche-Borghi
Contact telephone/fax/email:
Tel: ** 39 51 320 558 or 373 765
Fax: ** 39 51 320 960
Email: panzini@kidslink.bo.cnr.it

Also contact: Miriam Traversi, CD/LEI, Bologna (see case study 2.1 for further information)

The school caters for 11-14 year olds. There are 338 pupils on roll, 20% of whom are of ethnic minority origin, mainly of Chinese, Sinti, Former Yugoslavian (mainly Romany), Moroccan, Persian and Bulgarian origin. The school has a workshop and specific resources for teaching Italian as a second language. It is situated in a generally deprived working class area not far from a Reception Centre for new arrivals and near a camp for travellers which experienced an influx of people from southern Italy in the 1970s. These people have now generally reached a reasonable level of economic prosperity and social inclusion. The more recent ethnic minority settlers experience socio-economic disadvantage and are subject to racial discrimination. It is the children of these families who attend the school.

Aims of the multi-level work

- to improve the appreciation and valuing of different cultures by bringing pupils closer together to learn from first-hand experience of different cultures, exploring these cultures with them and enabling them to understand the value of diversity

- to provide in-service training for teachers and other staff and develop projects which promote and develop intercultural education in the school and community

- to raise the achievement levels of ethnic minority pupils through an integrated approach, involving other schools (of the same and different phases or levels) and agencies, with a particular emphasis on the learning of Italian as a second language

- to raise achievement levels through involving parents in learning Italian as an additional language

- to promote pilot projects in co-operation with primary and upper secondary schools, with the aim of improving pupils' participation levels in upper secondary education.

Panzini-Zappa emphasises continuing education and training for its teachers. Staff refresher courses on intercultural issues have developed from lectures and presentations to interactive workshops which produce lesson plans and teaching and learning materials. This change in methodology is helping teachers to develop their ways of working in the classrooms and helps them deal with new situations in a flexible but effective way. This mirrors the school's efforts to couple quality and effectiveness of teaching with meeting the everyday needs thrown up by increasing diversity in the classroom.

Panzini-Zappa lobbies actively for provision of more specialised language workshops in more schools. It recognises the crucial importance of addressing the language needs of newly arrived pupils who are learning Italian as a second language. A multi-level pilot project has just started. Promoted by the Provincial Education Authority of Bologna, it has pedagogical guidance from CD/LEI (see page 47) and will be monitored and evaluated on an on-going basis by the Department of Education of the University of Bologna in collaboration with a Statistics Unit and under the supervision of CD/LEI.

Parents are closely involved in the initiatives promoted by the school. Panzini-Zappa regards this as crucial to the achievement of the pupils. In March 1998 the school set up one of three new 'parents' rooms' established in schools in Bologna. Here, parents will participate in the pilot project on teaching Italian as a second language.

All the initiatives set up by Panzini-Zappa are **characterised** by the move to involve other agencies and parents in devising and developing projects and the need to collaborate with other agencies to improve competence and understanding, share common concerns and approaches and value differences. Panzini-Zappa collaborates specifically with

- other schools in the same phase of education and in different phases (primary, upper secondary)

- inter-institutional and multi-disciplinary centres (for example, CD/LEI)

- the University of Bologna

- ethnic minority communities and their leaders

- parents and guardians of children

- other support services of the City of Bologna (for example, Social Services)

- private agencies providing support for educational technology.

The school is led by a headteacher who has clear vision, provides transparent and fair leadership and has good understanding of a wide range of pedagogical issues, including those relating to intercultural education and the needs of ethnic minority pupils, and a strong commitment to these areas of work. Communications within the school and between the school and its partners are excellent, and the school is committed to a range of positive actions on a number of fronts.

What has been learned?
- the location of the school in the geographical centre of its communities is helpful

- it is important to create local networks and partnerships with a wide range of people, services and organisations which can enhance the education and learning of pupils from ethnic minority backgrounds

- consistent effort must be sustained to involve the ethnic minority communities

- the school is conscious of the need to involve its pupils in a wide range of activities outside the normal school curriculum and is increasingly involved with sports organisations, the university, centres for intercultural education such as CD/LEI – all of which assist the school in responding to the needs of an increasingly diverse pupil population.

Main outcomes

Pupils: the involvement of their parents, the process of valuing and recognising their home language and culture and the positive response to their needs create a supportive learning environment which enhances pupils' self-esteem and self-confidence. Their language skills and acquisition of Italian as a second language are supported by the language workshop. There is now a focus on the academic and technical language needed for success in the school curriculum. Particular attention is also paid to the pupils' social and personal development.

Teachers: teachers find that their sense of responsibility and motivation is enhanced at a time when they are also having to cope with a major change towards greater school autonomy. There is considerable emphasis on professional development which gives teachers greater confidence in meeting the needs of ethnic minority pupils; there is a real sense in which professional development is helping the teachers to learn and grow alongside the pupils, with the support of the headteacher, and alongside the parents and local communities.

The school: the school is growing as a whole learning community. Its awareness of issues and how to respond to them is increasing, as is the range of strategies it can use to respond to diversity. The multi-level working is a major help with these processes.

Parents: parents of ethnic minority pupils are using the parents' room for a number of purposes, among them to make their views heard about the needs of their children. Panzini-Zappa is aiming in the short term to involve as many parents as possible in these developments, as it recognises the clear benefits for the pupils' progress. Parents who speak Italian as their first language and those from different backgrounds are learning to work together as a result of attending the parents' room activities and beginning to realise how much they have in common, especially in relation to the welfare of their children.

Implications for in-service training

- teachers need to be trained in pedagogy, educational methodology, working with children and young people etc. At present their degree programme prepares them only in terms of the content of their subject area or disciplines

- because of the increasing level of diversity in classrooms, there is a constant need to raise teachers' awareness and sensitivity to intercultural issues and to enable them to mediate between people from diverse backgrounds

- teachers need to be trained in how they can interact successfully with ethnic minority parents

- there is a need to extend teachers' theoretical understanding and methodological skills in teaching language, including the teaching of Italian as a second or additional language

- teachers need to be trained to respond to the challenges of diversity in the classroom and to their changing role in a changing school system. As well as the demands of moves towards school autonomy, teachers find that more and more developments are of a 'top-down' nature, and this does not motivate them as much as being involved in initiatives which arise from their own interests. There is a need for a better balance of 'bottom-up' and 'top-down' developments.

Case Study 3.4

Multi-level working in Motala, Sweden

Name of School: Rassnasskolan, Motala, Sweden

Headteacher: Britt Brostrom

Contact telephone / fax / email:

Tel: ** 46 141 225 743

Fax: ** 46 141 554 57

Email: britt@mbox310.swipnet

The 1994 requirement in Swedish Law for the curriculum in schools says:

> The main task of the school is to impart knowledge and understanding and **together with the home**, help pupils develop into responsible persons and members of society. **The school shall help families by supporting them in their role of bringing up and developing their children**. As a result there **must be close co-operation between the school and home...** The school shall stimulate each pupil towards self-development and personal growth **...Every pupil has the right to develop in school, to feel the joy of growth and experience the satisfaction that comes from making progress and overcoming difficulties**.

Thus, many of the ideas developed within the DIECEC Network are required of Swedish schools in response to this legislation, especially the involvement of parents and an effective response to diversity. The Rassnasskolan has a school development plan for achieving these goals through the curriculum of the school. The school has 550 pupils and is divided into three sections, with each section having pupils from age 6 – 12. About 25% of the pupils speak Swedish as a second language, which causes difficulties in terms of effective communications with parents, but the school uses interpreters wherever possible.

There is a multi-level approach in the school in terms of the involvement of staff, parents and pupils. **The staff** consists of teachers, pre-school teachers and 'fritidspedagoger' (staff with high level pedagogical training but no teaching qualification). The fritidspedagoger work with the children in their leisure time and form a link between out of school hours activities and school lessons; they work as a team alongside the teachers in school and with the children during the afternoons.

The parents are represented on a Parents Council. There is a separate Council for each of the three sections of the school, so a broad range of parents can be involved. Staff representatives attend meetings of the Council with parents to discuss how the school can be improved regarding finance, the school grounds, resources, festivals, the curriculum, special projects etc.

The pupils also have a Council for each part of the school and for each year group to consider how to improve conditions for them at school, the lunch breaks, their schoolwork etc. Where possible, their suggestions are acted on.

These three levels also come together to support the progress of each child. The parents are invited to the school at least twice a year and sometimes several times, to discuss together with their child and the classteacher or mentor the whole development of the child. The aim is to find ways of supporting the child's progress and achievement at school and at home through including the work of the 'fritidspedagoger'. An agreement is recorded about what the school, the parents and the child will do before the next meeting. The child is the subject of these discussions but is always involved in them.

Aims of the multi-level and multi-agency work

Since 1995 there is a developing multi-agency network in the western part of Motala. The aims of this co-operation go beyond education and include:

- improving the community health profile of the people living in the area through inter-agency co-operation

- prioritising work with children, young people and their families in the first instance

- addressing the particular needs of ethnic minority children and their families

The Rassnasskolan has certain **specific** activities and processes. One team of people works on language development, of both monolingual and emergent bilingual children. The children's mother tongue is supported as well as their acquisition of Swedish as a second language. Another team deals with working with ethnic minority parents as partners in supporting the education of their children, and a further team works in a project which offers a range of leisure-time activities to children between 8 and 9, to support their learning and development outside normal school hours.

This development is characterised by:

- multi-level working within the school in ways which involve parents, teachers and pupils in developing a supportive framework for the children's education

- multi-agency working around the school and the families, to try to ensure that there is good support for their general development as well as their education

- clear leadership in the school over the importance of multi-level working.

What has been learned?

- by working together all partners can achieve their aims more easily

- it takes time and effort to build an effective partnership and it needs to be maintained and developed

- it is difficult to persuade politicians to understand the benefits and to organise their political work in ways which reflect this approach, but you have to keep on trying!

- it is harder to see things from a 'bottom-up' perspective in which all the people and services are there to support the child, as opposed to a traditional 'top-down' model

- it can be difficult to work in a partnership and to help others to achieve the goals rather than trying to do it all yourself. This is especially true when working with parents so that the school is really supporting them rather than simply expecting something of them which they may not be able to do. But it is ultimately the only lasting and effective approach.

- we need to learn far more about different cultural, religious and linguistic backgrounds so we can understand our children and their parents better and respond more effectively to their needs.

Main outcomes

Self-esteem and empowerment: the democratic working structures established (Parents' and Pupils' Councils) help to empower people. Under these circumstances, the levels of responsibility and degree of influence of the pupils increases. The fact that pupils' views are listened to and acted upon, and that their work and achievements are recognised and valued, helps to support their self-esteem. The same applies to parents.

Basic skills: ethnic minority pupils' command of basic skills, especially literacy, have improved as a result of a specific programme on literacy which includes Reading Recovery. The parents are involved in this work and it is paying dividends. There are considerable improvements in the literacy levels of the pupils from entry into school to the end of their second year of statutory education.

Personal and social development: close co-operation between school and home pays huge dividends. The school has no specific data on this, but observations suggest that the involvement of parents is a key factor in supporting personal and social development – and so is the work of the *fritidspedagoger*.

Implications for in-service training

- training is needed in how to work in a multi-agency partnership and in working effectively with parents, especially those from different backgrounds

- it is important to train people so that they understand and respect each other's roles and expertise

- further training is needed in how to support children's literacy and numeracy development and how to use a wider range of teaching methodologies – this is brought into sharper focus once a school has to respond to the needs of a diverse population or to one which differs in terms of cultural, faith and linguistic background from the teachers.

Rassnasskolan has started a project called 'Internationalism' and one section of the school has been working on this theme for two years. It is now becoming a project for the whole school. It is important to have an international perspective, to be able to see one's own reality in a global context in order to create international solidarity and prepare pupils for a society which will have closer cross-cultural and cross-border contacts.

Case Study 3.5

De Notenkraker School, Rotterdam

Name of School: De Notenkraker, Rotterdam

Headteacher: Anton de Jong

Contact telephone/fax/email:

Tel: ** 31 10 295 7273

Fax: ** 31 10 295 7273

Email: aajung@worldonline.nl

De Notenkraker is a primary school catering for 240 children in a deprived area in the centre of Hoogvliet, a suburb of Rotterdam. It has a diverse pupil population: 40% of the pupils are from ethnic minority backgrounds whose first language is not Dutch.

The school is one of the 'Brede School' (Partner Schools) in Rotterdam. This means that it seeks to operate as a hub of education and learning within its community, and to support the education of its pupils, parents and other adults living in the community, by supporting education at school, at home and in the community. Also central to the concept of the school is the importance of children being ready to learn, having good levels of self-esteem and believing that they can succeed. It is also a Digital School. It has a good level of information and communications technology equipment and these facilities are well used during and after the school day. The school is open for 52 weeks per year, from early in the morning until late in the evenings, including weekends. There is a wide range of educational, recreational and leisure activities available to children and adults at the school outside the normal school day.

A significant number of adults other than teachers, including a good number of young people, work at the school, especially in the evenings but also in class-support roles. Some of them are volunteers; some of them are funded by a government scheme to encourage people back into work; some are paid for by the school from its budget. All are part of the 'team' of adults at the school and in the eyes of the headteacher they all have an important part to play in the provision of education at the school; it is significant that all the staff are accorded the same degree of respect and support.

There is a Police Station on the school site! The image of this station is quite different from the normal image. The police have a positive presence in and around the school; parents visiting the school enter through the Police Station, which also serves as the reception office for the school. Crime and vandalism, and other anti-social activity, have greatly reduced in the area since De Notenkraker developed as a Partner School. The school site has been developed so that the outside areas are available for a variety of sports and games, and there is an indoor sports facility.

Multi-level working

The school is able to operate a wide range of additional activities and work successfully with the parents and children, because it has established, maintained and developed a large number of productive partnerships with people, services, organisations and funding bodies.

The headteacher takes the view that parents have skills, knowledge, understanding and interests which can help their child and other children to develop. Parents organise and present activities at the school during and outside the school day – often on a voluntary basis. Parents are also involved as learners in activities organised by other parents and by a range of other organisations.

The work of the school is also underpinned by partnerships with significant local and civic strategic bodies: the Municipal Council in Hoogvliet, the Rotterdam Education Service, the Urban Regeneration Office, the Welfare Foundation and others; representatives of these organisations make up a Steering Committee for the school with which the headteacher works closely. There is also an advisory group made up of representatives of the local community, including the parents and community associations.

There are also significant partnerships with services which provide support for individual children and those who are vulnerable or in some way 'at risk'. Some of the partnerships indicated above also play an important role in this co-ordination of the work of different services and agencies which support such children and their families.

The **aims** of the approach at De Notenkraker are:

- to improve the educational levels of pupils

- to raise their self-esteem and self-confidence and show them that they can be successful

- to involve parents and other adults in the community in activities which enable them to develop and which help the children to achieve; within this, there is a focus on the active and productive use of leisure time

- to improve children's and adults' social skills and their ability to value and appreciate diversity

- to raise the self-esteem of the whole community and improve the quality of life in the area.

The school's engagement with a wide range of partners who support the children's education and use of leisure time requires a good deal of liaison work, meetings and communication. The time this demands is a major issue, as is continuity of funding for activities. As a pilot 'Partner School', De Notenkraker received little additional funding to enable these processes to be put in place and the school has been actively seeking additional funds for activities at the school. This has put a strain on the headteacher's time, however, and raises the question of how much school staff should or can be involved in the implementation of the multi-level approach beyond their responsibility to ensure high quality education in the school and develop the engagement of parents. The experiences of schools like De Notenkraker suggests that a co-ordinator is needed at neighbourhood or area level, especially where there are several schools serving the communities living there. In the case of De Notenkraker, other primary schools and the secondary school in the area could benefit from a neighbourhood co-ordination arrangement.

This development is characterised by:
- a multi-level approach which scaffolds children's, young people's and adults' learning and use of leisure time

- the availability of extensive educational and recreational activities at the school throughout the day, week and year

- the involvement of a wide range of partners in steering the work at the school, providing and funding the activities

- the involvement of parents and other adults as teachers and tutors, not just as learners

- the positive presence of a police station on the school premises

- a clear educational effect on the school community, but also a broader effect on the quality of life in the neighbourhood and on community safety.

What has been learned?
The increase in the teachers' workload has not been so great – if anything, they can concentrate more on their teaching. The headteacher is fortunate to have enough resources to allow his deputy headteacher to more or less run the school on a day-to-day basis. His role has changed: he is acting more and more as the coordinator of education in the community. This has many implications, for example:

- the training of headteachers in the future for work of this kind

- the ways in which resources can be brought together to implement a whole community approach to education

- the need to have people with a similar vision and understanding working at city, school and neighbourhood levels

- the need for these visions or ideas to continue to develop: it is important not to develop a concept and then set it in concrete

- the need for long-term evaluation based on outcomes for children, young people, parents and the whole community.

The availability of information technology hardware and software for use beyond school hours as well as during them is a factor in providing a wide range of opportunities for learning. Parents can benefit from access to these facilities in ways which help to improve their employability.

Main outcomes

- there is considerable evidence that the quality of education in the school has been enhanced by its development as a 'Partner School'

- there is greater appreciation among the parents of the work and role of the school and of the importance of education to them and their children

- considerable numbers of children and parents attend and benefit from the activities which are organised beyond school hours

- as well as an overall effect on achievement, attendance and other outcomes for the children, there are many examples of individual children and adults benefiting in various ways from the development of the school

- there has been a noticeable effect on the quality of life and on community safety in the neighbourhood

- police perceptions of the community and community perceptions of the police have both become more positive

- partnerships are in place which can ensure the further development of the school.

Implications for in-service training

- working as a partner school requires training for teaching staff in terms of their role. Training is also needed in how to work with other organisations and with parents, especially when parents are from a different background in terms of race, language, culture, faith or socio-economic factors

- headteachers and potential headteachers of schools operating in this way need training in the implications for their role, its extent, how it can be managed and how to establish and manage partnerships; indeed, everyone involved in the schools has to be prepared to learn

- initial teacher training needs to prepare teachers for working in partner schools

- tutors, parents and other people providing educational and recreational activities in a partner school need training and support to ensure that they can meet their own expectations and those of the children and adults they are working with

- child protection and other issues of security have to be addressed.

Case Study 3.6

Hojstrupskolen, Odense, Denmark

Headteacher: Per Mathiesen
Contact telephone / fax / email:
Tel: ** 45 66 168 799
Fax: ** 45 66 169 865

The Hojstrupskole was built in 1956 in the western part of the Danish city of Odense. In 1998/99 there were 350 children aged from 6 to 12 on roll, 110 of them biligual or emergent bilingual. In 1992 Project Hojstrup was started – a multi-level project involving staff from the Public Welfare Office, the Youth/Continuation School (Ungdomsskole) and Hojstrupskolen. In recent years the number of refugee and other children from ethnic minority backgrounds has increased and continues to grow. At the same time, the number of children with Danish as their first language has reduced because some Danish parents opt for monocultural schools.

In 1994, the Danish Ministry of Education, the Ministry of Social Affairs and the City Development Department offered the chance to run an 'integration project'. In co-operation with the local 'Ungdomsskole' (Youth School), a Housing Co-operative and the Social Welfare Office we applied for a multi-agency project in an attempt to improve conditions for education and general development at school and also at home and in time out of school hours. We applied for a project with six elements to it:

- a mathematics project focusing on pre-school children

- a better school start project for children in the first three years of schooling (aged 6-9)

- a collaborative project to prevent failure at school for 9 – 13 year olds, called *Blaeksprutten* – 'The Octopus'

- a mother tongue teaching project

- a leisure-time project for 9-16 year-olds

- a project to enable parents to use school facilities.

Later, a cafe project for parents and children was established in the neighbourhood.

We have implemented these elements over two to four years and are now looking for ways to continue those which work best. This case study focuses on projects in the school. Hojstrup works on the basis that children who have too many problems on their minds often lack the strength or concentration to learn. Hojstrup places the emphasis on preventative, collaborative work, seeking to tackle problems when they are small and it is easier to co-operate with parents – and crucially, before the children have lost faith in themselves

Aims of the multi-level work

*   to reduce the number of children and young people removed from their homes, reduce youth crime and the number of children and young people who are expelled from or drop out of school

*   to give the children, through process-oriented school projects, knowledge and strength which enables them to determine their own identity

*   to involve in particular socially vulnerable children and young people in construc-tive activities as an alternative to their turbulent existence

*   to organise special programmes for children and young people and their families related to abuse and criminality

*   to involve the local further education college in out-reach work in the local com-munity. To achieve this aim, the head of the project and the head of the college will co-operate in providing alternative educational opportunities and the social activities of the college will be reinforced.

The project has two elements:

1. '*Octopus*': to support and develop the child's and parent's ability to structure their lives through an early preventative programme. The target group is children and families 'at risk' in the Hojstrupskolen area. The measures include support from counsellors for the family and in school time, and work in smaller groups for the children (4-6 pupils in a group).

An interdisiplinary team identifies a contact person to work with the family – there should be one person who relates to the family consistently so they are not over-whelmed by large numbers of unfamiliar people calling on them! If it is agreed that the family would benefit from involvement in the project, they and the contact person agree an action plan covering provision at school for the children/child, spare time (oppor-tunities to attend sports, music, other cultural activities), and support for the family as a unit, providing resources to help the family keep to the action plan, review progress etc.

This action plan is the core of the project. The project team help it to work – it may mean escorting a child to an out-of-school activity, teaching the family how to do so, offering a framework for whole family activities. Much of this depends on the project team establishing an agreed set of values. The action plan has now been developed so that it also functions as a contract or agreement between the school, the parents and the child.

2. *The Mother Tongue Project*: Emergent bilingual pupils often experience difficulties when the range of subjects is increased as they move through the school system. New subjects require an understanding of difficult concepts which are explained in technical and academic language unfamiliar to pupils learning Danish as a second language. The school applied for additional funding to support ethnic minority pupils' language development and was granted sufficient for 100 additional teaching hours plus a Turkish mother tongue teacher. These resources are aimed:

- to improve access for emergent bilingual pupils to technical and academic language by using both mother tongue and second language

- to create a good working relationship between the mother tongue teacher and the other teachers, and rationalise the curriculum which has to be taught and the curriculum for the mother tongue classes

- to enable the other teachers to see the mother tongue teaching as a resource and the teacher as an equal partner

- to create opportunities for parents to help their children with homework by enabling children to use their mother tongue to understand concepts before learning them in Danish

- to disseminate experiences and teaching and learning resources to other mother tongue teachers and teachers operating in Danish.

The project has worked through a number of stages – forming working groups, meeting with parents to explain the project to them, identifying specific problems in individual subjects, producing teaching and learning materials (sometimes involving parents), testing and evaluating the materials, presenting the materials to parents and disseminating them among teachers in Odense, including other mother tongue teachers.

This development is characterised by:
- a multi-disciplinary and multi-level approach to preventing school failure and supporting children's and young people's education at school, at home and in leisure time

- a focus on six specific themes or elements, all of which reflect major themes identified by DIECEC as contributing to a successful approach with ethnic minority pupils and their parents

- the planning, implementation and evaluation of specific, concrete activities with complementary aims.

What has been learned?

- multi-level working is a vital approach to catering more successfully for pupils from ethnic minority backgrounds

- multi-level working is important not just for children and young people at risk but also for any group of pupils who are in danger of underachieving at school

- support for children's learning and development in the contexts of home, school and community/leisure time is essential

- to ensure that this support is effective, a wide range of partners needs to be involved; these partners have to sort out their arrangements for working with each other so they co-operate effectively

- mother tongue teaching needs to be closely linked to the curriculum demands of subjects and to specific, identified difficulties caused by programmes of study; the development of the mother tongue and of the second language are mutually supportive where the teaching processes and the content of the lessons are closely linked.

Implications for in-service training

- successful multi-level working means that people from different professional backgrounds need to be trained together so that they have a mutual understanding of and respect for each other's roles

- all people working with ethnic minority children and their families need to have a good understanding of their cultural backgrounds

- subject and class teachers need to understand the processes of language acquisition and to be enabled to work in close partnership with specialists who teach mother tongues and the second or additional languages.

SECTION FOUR
MULTI-LEVEL WORKING IN THE THEMES OF INTERCULTURAL EDUCATION AND RAISING ACHIEVEMENT

Introduction

The eight themes in Section Four are as follows:

A. Teaching and learning second or additional languages

B. Teaching and learning mother tongues

C. Improving basic skills: literacy, numeracy and information and communications technology

D. Engaging parents as prime educators of their children

E. Additional opportunities for learning

F. Intercultural understanding and antiracist measures

G. Provision for children from cradle to school and for their parents

H. Provision for children and young people at risk of failure: second chance schooling

I. Pathways to Further and Higher Education, Training and Employment

Each theme consists of an introduction and a number of case studies. The themes are by no means exhaustive but all have been identified as priorities by the DIECEC cities, which have proved that multi-level working within these themes promote intercultural education and the achievement levels of ethnic minority pupils. It has not been possible to include all the case studies offered by the cities, only a representative sample of work in different parts of the European Union.

The experience of DIECEC cities has been that not everything can be done at once. It is better to prioritise a few themes at a time, whether this is at whole education system, neighbourhood or individual school level.

Theme A
Teaching and Learning – second or additional languages

The interrelationship of mother-tongue and second or additional language learning and the need for high levels of competence in both

A fluent and in-depth command of the language of the city and country in which children live is a prerequisite for success in its education system. Whatever people's views about the education system and its suitability for ethnic minority pupils, it is unlikely to change rapidly. For the young people in it now and the immediate future, the issue is to be able to succeed within the existing system. The sooner pupils become competent in the dominant language of the city, the better. The nature of this 'high level of competence' is discussed below.

Almost all children already have some oral competence in one or more languages when they start school. DIECEC cities know that good command of the mother tongue supports rapid acquisition of subsequent languages, and vice-versa. So work on this theme has to be considered alongside work on Theme B (Teaching and Learning Mother Tongues). DIECEC has impressive evidence that children make rapid progress where teaching their mother tongue is suitably integrated with teaching the second language.

International research supports this view of the positive interaction of mother tongue and second or additional language. DIECEC rejects completely the notion that learning more than one language is difficult, especially for children. As the case studies often illustrate, children and adults alike make better progress in their acquisition of an additional language if they have a good and developing command of their mother tongue but schools, cities and education systems have to be clear about what bilingualism entails.

DIECEC is concerned about the word 'bilingual' being used in some cities and countries to describe children who are in the process of acquiring more than one language. Describing them so in the early stages of this process is to misunderstand the importance of the notion of bilingualism. Bilingualism implies a high level of competence in two languages, not merely getting by in them at a basic level. While the level of command required to be considered bilingual is difficult to define, it certainly embraces being able to use both languages for the purposes of learning, rational thought and argument, expressing complex ideas and using the language to develop further competence in it. It is misleading to use the word 'bilingual' to describe children and young people who have only low-level command of either, both or all of their languages. The phrases 'becoming bilingual', 'emergent bilingual' or 'potentially bilingual' are more accurate and less open to misinterpretation.

Approaches to teaching and learning which use, value and develop both languages to high levels are therefore important in this theme. No one approach to teaching and learning will guarantee success for all children (and we have to aim for a guarantee of success). Only operating a system of withdrawal or separate groups to teach the second language is as inappropriate as only operating a system of in-class support regardless of the different starting points and needs of pupils. In contexts where pupils are using two or more languages on a daily basis at least during school time, approaches in schools which ban the use of the mother tongue or relegate it to an inferior position will not be as successful as models which develop both languages in parallel – quite apart from the effects on pupils' self-esteem and readiness to learn.

Becoming fluent in mother tongue and second language

International research demonstrates that children can acquire a superficial command of a language fairly quickly (sometimes within six months, or more commonly in eighteen months to two years), but also – crucially **that their acquisition of a second or additional language must be effectively scaffolded for between five and seven years**.

Superficial command of the language of the school and state should never be accepted as sufficient. Emergent bilingual or multilingual children can end up by being 'semi-lingual' in two or more languages and fail to develop sufficient command of any language to use it for reasoning and learning. They have limited vocabulary (sometimes referred to as 'survival' language), confuse structures between languages and have not mastered the technical and academic language they need to succeed at school. They may not have been taught to differentiate between the dialect forms which they use with their peers in everyday social interactions, and the technical and academic language required for academic success.

One test of children's competence and confidence in a particular language is how well they can explain their learning, using the appropriate technical language to other children and adults, verbally and ultimately in written presentations. Teachers and other adults need to help children to understand that correct use of language is vital. The appropriate forms of language have to be illustrated to children so that they come to regard precise and accurate language not as a form of snobbery, but as a tool for success. They will have to cope later with further and higher education or employment interviews and particularly with written and oral examinations. A frequent barrier to higher achievement in terms of success in assessments and examinations is the disparity between many ethnic minority children's knowledge and understanding and their ability to express their knowledge fully in appropriate language, especially in writing.

Teachers can certainly value dialect and non-standard usage as a means of appropriate oral communication among peers but need to be consistently clear about the importance of correct technical usage where it is required.

There are proven key links between language acquisition and cognitive development: poor acquisition and use of language inhibits cognitive development, resulting in a standstill or even regression in learning. Close correlation has been found between poor language development and low self-esteem, especially for ethnic minority children and children from educationally disadvantaged backgrounds. Children, especially the younger ones, who spend much of their time in school on tasks which have little interaction with a skilled language user may suffer a double penalty: slower or inhibited language development and less rapid cognitive development. These findings must inform the debate about the nature of the early years and lower primary curriculum.

Rapid and 'deep' development of the mother tongue and the second or additional language is essential to educational and personal achievement. 'Deep' development means:

- having command and an innate or developed understanding of the deeper structures of language

- understanding alternative meanings, including idiomatic and technical meanings

- having the skills to use these elements of language to express complex ideas and concepts accurately

- being able to use language to reason and argue

- being able to use language to acquire further knowledge and understanding

- being able to differentiate between different meanings of the same words according to the context in which they are used.

Without these higher order language skills, children and young people will be seriously disadvantaged in their learning.

Developing higher level language skills

DIECEC cities take different approaches, ranging from apparently inclusive, in-class support models (typically with a class or subject teacher working alongside a 'language support' teacher) which claim to provide access to the whole curriculum, regardless of pupils' levels of competence in their mother tongue or additional language, through to separate 'preparatory' or 'induction' classes for most or all of the curriculum time for up to two years for children whose mother tongue is not that of the city. What counts is which approaches – in terms of organisational arrangements and, crucially, pedagogy, including teaching methodology – work best for securing the pupils' overall educational progress and achievement levels.

The following case studies illustrate some of these different contexts and approaches. DIECEC does not recommend one above another, but certain general conclusions about the nature of provision and methodology can be drawn:

Quality of teaching

*   Teaching potentially bilingual children is a high level, specialist skill which requires specific training; it is not the case that any teacher or support teacher can teach such children successfully. Teachers need specialised knowledge, skills and understanding, and a positive attitude to ethnic minority pupils and the advantages of genuine bilingualism, and they must themselves use language skilfully. All teachers and support staff working with ethnic minority children must have specific training and appropriate qualifications or be engaged in training as they gain experience of working with them in the company of a trained specialist.

*   In the early stages of additional language acquisition, intensive teaching and learning in small groups while expecting high levels of achievement, pays dividends. Teachers need to model language appropriately and know how to use children's miscue and error as a source of learning and improvement. Engaging children in meaningful talk, backed up by appropriate resources and stimuli, is a fundamental feature of good practice. Young learners of second or additional languages need frequent and consistent opportunities to acquire and use their languages with a skilled adult user and teacher. DIECEC still sees too many children having too few opportunities to develop active use of their languages, especially in their first few years of education.

*   Children and young people need endless opportunities to practice their newly experienced language with support from skilled adults and (increasingly as they progress) other pupils. Mistakes should be seen as opportunities to learn and remodel language; this 'reinforcement' stage has to be

supported by appropriate learning resources, for example, representations of key words and phrases with definitions or contextual clues to their precise meaning. This stage will also involve reference to alternative meanings of words and phrases.

- Pupils need opportunities to extend their understanding and use of newly acquired language. They need to be encouraged and helped by teachers to seek out different meanings of words, to learn to explain these differences and to speculate about how they might have come about.

- Pupils must be required to 'perform' orally and in writing so as to both demonstrate and refine their learning. They need such opportunities to use new and previously acquired language, to develop confidence and (through skilful questioning by teachers and other pupils guided by teachers) the ability to manipulate language in increasingly sophisticated ways. In all the pupils' learning activities what is vital is the ability of teachers and other adults to model language and ask questions which invite and elicit responses appropriate to the competence and confidence of the pupils. It is this skill and understanding which teachers need to develop through a combination of training and classroom experience.

This is no easy task, especially with large classes of children and for non-specialist teachers. Arrangements such as those described below, which reduce class sizes or split classes for all or part of the school day and deploy specialist teachers with these smaller groups, are a particularly effective use of additional resources in the early years of children's language learning.

Aspects of organisation

- Teachers need a curriculum framework for the acquisition of the second or additional language which broadly sets out the areas of vocabulary, idiom, structure and technical or academic language which children should have acquired by certain key points. This framework is best organised on a national or at least regional or city basis. It will help to ensure a reasonable degree of commonality of expectations and save teachers much valuable planning and evaluation time.

- There is no one correct or 'best' arrangement in terms of inclusive or more separate lessons – different arrangements are appropriate at different times and stages of language acquisition. If, for example, a child or group of children are really struggling to acquire a basic command, giving them intensive teaching by themselves for as long as is necessary ought to be perfectly acceptable.

- Teachers and schools need a variety of strategies and arrangements to hand and ways of identifying which are appropriate for which children at different times.

- Bilingual approaches which involve children operating in both their mother tongue and their second or additional language can work well, as long as teachers are clear about their learning objectives and outcomes for the children. Children spend less than 15% of their time in school, so if school is virtually the only place where they speak and learn this additional language, these learning outcomes have to be focused on its rapid and 'deep' acquisition, alongside further development of the mother tongue. This is a highly skilled and demanding task – a further reason why this work depends for its success on highly trained staff.

The introduction of formal literacy skills – a question of timing

There is considerable debate and controversy within DIECEC over the optimal point to introduce children to the more formal aspects of literacy acquisition, especially reading and writing. The research evidence demonstrates that developing literacy skills in the mother tongue supports literacy acquisition in the second or additional language, and vice versa.

There are two basic schools of thought and practice. One, based mainly in the Scandinavian cities, sees the main aims of the early years of education, certainly up to age 6, as follows:

- development of social skills and socialisation processes

- development to as high a level as possible of speaking and listening skills

- experience of a wide range of 'hands-on' activities covering all aspects of early childhood development and 'areas of experience'

- development of gross and fine motor skills, partly in preparation for writing

- development of enjoyment in participating in group activities and in learning.

At one extreme, schools will say that they prefer children to enter school at 6 with no reading or writing skills at all – but with the skills above highly developed. They argue: 'give us children who have had these experiences and developed these basic skills, and we will teach them to read and write when they start statutory schooling or shortly after that – but certainly not before they are 6'. Interestingly, the systems which adopt this approach often out-perform those which begin formal literacy learning earlier. The point at which children start to out-perform those who have an earlier start with formal literacy seems to be around the age of 9 or 10.

The other approach, adopted for instance in the UK, introduces formal literacy skills much earlier, on the grounds that reading and writing are vital basic skills and children can undoubtedly cope. Key questions here are:

- are some children being asked to become literate before they have acquired sufficient competence and confidence as speakers and listeners (and particularly, a sufficient grasp of meaning)?

- do children who make this early start miss out on important aspects of early childhood development?

- do the positive effects of early literacy learning outweigh these disadvantages?

These are particular issues for children learning the main language of the curriculum as a second or additional language. In DIECEC's view, the jury is still out! However a major danger in introducing formal literacy skills early is that some potentially bilingual children are not yet ready. The concept of 'readiness for literacy' is significant and schools should be able to decide, supported by good advice, when it is appropriate to begin teaching individual children to read and write. This is not a mark of low expectations or a question of delaying because children are perceived to have some sort of deficit. It is a matter of professional educational judgement based on evidence of some children being demotivated and regressing as a result of being forced into acquiring literacy skills too early to perform writing tasks for which they are still less ready.

At the same time, it is important not to deny children the opportunity to acquire literacy skills when they are ready to do so. Given that children have very different starting points in terms of their level of development when they start school, it would be less than logical to intoduce formal literacy learning to all children at the same time.

The reason for introducing these arguments here – as well as referring to them in Theme C: Basic Skills – is to point out that the introduction of formal literacy skills must not be allowed to inhibit children's acquisition of the skills of active listening and speaking, especially at a point where they are beginning to achieve a reasonable level of competence and confidence.

The specific case of new arrivals

By 'new arrivals' DIECEC means children who arrive in a city after the start of statutory schooling with varying degrees of experience of an education system and of competence in the majority language of their new home.

Assuming that assessment on arrival has been undertaken, the following principles ought to apply to provision:

- Teaching the second or additional language to these pupils is a specialist skill within the specialism of teaching second languages. The process of language acquisition has to be greatly accelerated for these pupils, so that they have genuine access to the curriculum as soon as possible.

- Cities and schools need to consider the extent to which it is possible and economically viable to make specialised provision available in all schools. This will depend on the number of new arrivals and the diversity of their backgrounds. It is better to resource a smaller number of schools to make specific and specialised provision for these pupils than to expect or allow all schools to do so. Where a system of parental choice or preference for schools operates, these arrangements will need to be explained carefully to parents and outcomes decided which do not infringe these rights or the pupils' right to rapid acquisition of their second or additional language.

- The schools with designated provision for new arrivals should aim, firstly, to enable these pupils to acquire their new language rapidly and effectively, using contexts appropriate to their age and educational experience and to the school curriculum and, secondly, to provide access to the normal curriculum which is compatible with their ability to engage with it.

These arrangements will involve some separate, intensive, highly skilled teaching which should accelerate the acquisition of the second language especially in the child's first year or two at the school. It may involve additional time at school and an extended school week. How much time is spent on the normal curriculum should be determined on an individual basis following skilled and frequent assessment. Older pupils especially (from the age of 7 or 8) make better progress under such arrangements than if they spend all the time in a mainstream class with language support. DIECEC sees no evidence that flexible arrangements of this kind limit equality of opportunity and access, or undermine self-esteem and confidence. However, the key factor is the quality of the teaching and the availability of highly skilled teachers.

Theme A: Case Study 1

Development work in Turin

Silvana Mosca – CIDISS, Turin
Fax: ** 39 011 542 874
Tel: ** 39 011 560 7425

People of ethnic minority origin have only recently come to Turin. There was considerable immigration from the South of Italy, but now there are significant numbers of children who speak languages other than Italian as their first language. Many speak little or no Italian on entry to school. Many families have poor economic circumstances and live in sub-standard housing.

Developing programmes and methodology for the teaching and learning of Italian has been a priority for Turin within its policy on diversity and has developed through pilot projects in the schools where it is most required. Turin has also led a significant DIECEC project on the teaching and learning of second languages, called REPEAT, and this approach has both informed and been informed by the practical work undertaken by teachers on the ground.

- Pilot schools were identified by the Education Inspector responsible for second language development. Each school has a language workshop with a specialist teacher trained by CIDISS, an education development and training centre funded by the regional, provincial and city authorities who co-operate in a number of areas of educational policy.

- The specialist teachers are given intensive training and opportunities to work with each other as well as with their colleagues in schools, who regard them as experts and sources of help with developing their own methodologies in the classroom.

- The workshops provide children who are learning Italian as a second or additional language with frequent and intensive opportunities to develop their Italian so that they can participate fully in the curriculum of their school. As well as using commercially available resources, teachers have developed their own. There is evidence that the work of specialist teachers of Italian has a positive effect on teaching and learning in normal classes.

- Parents of the children learning Italian as a second or additional language are involved in the workshops which run sessions for them, both to improve their command of Italian and to show them how and what their children are learning.

This development is multi-level

- it involves a partnership between the Province, on behalf of the National Education System, the city and the region

- it involves pupils, parents, teachers, inspectors/advisers and whole school policies

- the evaluation of the development is multi-level, reflecting the impact of the programmes on children, parents and the school.

The development is characterised by:

- developing specialist expertise in a carefully planned and structured way in keeping with its recent beginnings

- opportunities for the specialists to develop their own expertise further and to work with other teachers

- multi-level activity and multi-level evaluation underpinned by a clear theoretical framework and understanding of the interconnectivity of language and culture.

Implications for in-service training

- All teachers working with children learning second or additional languages need training in how they can help children to make rapid progress in their second language and continue to develop their mother tongue.

- There is a need for highly trained specialist teachers of second languages who can work effectively with children, especially in the early stages, and with other teachers.

- While much of this training should be focused on issues of language, cultural identity and knowledge and understanding of different cultures and faiths must also figure in training programmes; issues of language and culture cannot be separated.

- Training programmes must have a central core of theoretical knowledge and understanding about language acquisition and the interaction of the processes of learning more than one language. They must also have a strong practical element which develops effective methodology, underpinned by a curriculum framework which provides an appropriate degree of structure to the language learning and ensures that the specific language required by the school curriculum and by each subject area (mathematics, science, technology etc) is taught.

Theme A Case Study 2

Teaching Dutch as a second language for newcomers to Rotterdam: the Prisma Project

Paul Hoop
Tel: ** 31 10 206 7112
Fax: ** 31 10 206 7104
E-mail: p.hoop@dso.rotterdam.nl

Rotterdam continues to be a city of major immigration, with established communities from different ethnic backgrounds. There is still a steady stream of new arrivals, often refugees, as a result of previous immigration and of political conflicts and wars. Rotterdam has well over 120 identifiable different ethnic or linguistic groups; the number of new arrivals each year continues to rise. Many children of ethnic minority origin need specific support for the development of their Dutch through the school system. So the need for successful methodologies for teaching Dutch as a second language is great.

It is not uncommon for there to be ten or more different first languages spoken by the children in one class and this complicates the issue of mother tongue teaching in schools. However, Rotterdam has developed specific and successful policies and practices for the rapid acquisition of Dutch as a second language. The outcomes for children and young people in terms of their levels of competence in Dutch are generally good. This case study looks at the main characteristics of these programmes.

What is the PRISMA Project?

PRISMA is a programme for teaching Dutch to newly arrived primary aged children in Rotterdam. It consists of in-service training in the theory and practice of language acquisition and second language teaching, a curriculum framework which provides guidance to teachers on the content and methodology of teaching Dutch as a second language, and materials corresponding to different levels of competence for teachers and learners. It was developed after the evaluation of previous approaches to teaching Dutch as a second language indicated that children could make more rapid progress.

The PRISMA project was established by the Education Advisory Service in Rotterdam, an independent organisation which works on a contractual basis with the City of Rotterdam and other providers of education. PRISMA was developed as a co-operative initiative between the service and the different school boards responsible for statutory education in the primary sector in Rotterdam.

The PRISMA Programme aims

- to accelerate and deepen newly-arrived primary-aged children's acquisition of Dutch as a second language

- to provide a flexible framework of training, curriculum materials and planning which would help teachers to cope with the requirements of children from different backgrounds working at different levels in the same class

- to help newly-arrived children to adapt to and integrate with the Dutch system of Education

- to train increasing numbers of teachers as specialists in the teaching and learning of Dutch as a second language

- to ensure access to the curriculum as rapidly as possible, enabling children to understand and use the academic and technical language demanded in curriculum subjects.

The PRISMA Programme was developed by a group of professional linguists, teachers and education advisers. It drew on the experience and expertise of qualified people with an understanding of the theory and practice of language acquisition, the situation and needs of newly-arrived children, the training needs of teachers and the limitations and requirements of classroom organisation.

The programme involves specialist teachers who have been trained in the methodology and in using the materials. The teachers are located in a number of primary schools throughout Rotterdam in order to concentrate expertise and make the best use of resources. Children who need support for their development in Dutch are assessed on their arrival and their parents made aware of the nearest school where the provision is available. The children spend each morning at the school which provides the specialist programme and the afternoon at their local school if this school does not provide the PRISMA programme.

The teaching groups are small – usually no more than twelve children – but the teacher has to work with a diverse group, possibly working at several different levels. The emphasis in the classes is on high quality interaction between the teacher and the pupils, in small groups or on an individual basis. Teachers assess pupils' progress on an on-going basis and they move through the different levels of the programme at different rates.

This development is characterised by:
- a programme informed by professional expertise in language acquisition, teaching and learning and the situation of newly-arrived children

- a multi-level approach which engages people with different but complementary areas of expertise

- a high level of expectation of the competence in a second language which children can achieve relatively quickly

- a focus on the teaching of Dutch as a second language as a specialist skill requiring specific knowledge and understanding

- a programme which provides specialist training, resources and planning materials linked to the different levels of pupils in the group and pathways which enable children to progress rapidly.

Implications for in-service training
- it is essential to have a flexible but clear programme which enables teachers to identify the most appropriate next steps for children

- even with small teaching groups, the different needs of children in the same group requires teachers to be very skillful and well prepared

- the fact that some children attend the classes in a different school from their main school does not seem to impede their access to the curriculum or their social development; rather, the rapid and effective way in which they acquire Dutch gives them much better access and they can interact with more children.

- teachers of second languages require specialist training to equip them with the theoretical background, knowledge and practical skills required to accelerate children's acquisition of additional languages

- such programmes are best designed and provided by experts who have strong theoretical understanding and also practical experience of implementation

- there is an important spin-off from the work of specialist teachers to other teachers working with emergent bilingual pupils.

Theme A: Case Study 3

AIMS Project – teaching and learning English as a second/additional language at Whetley First School, Bradford

Bradford, Whetley First School, Headteacher, Ron Braithwaite
Teachers: Yasmin Ali and Karen Westcott
Tel: ** 44 1274 543 711
Fax: ** 44 1274 547 939

Whetley First School is a co-educational inner city school with a predominantly Pakistani origin Muslim pupil population of around 380. Although there is a trend towards greater competence in English on entry to school, a majority of children still arrive in the nursery class with little English at age 3+. The school was concerned that the chilxdren would not be able to deal with the demands of the curriculum.

The school has ten bilingual staff and this has contributed to the range and effectiveness of the strategies for improving oracy. A visit to Amsterdam provided inspiration and challenges for the headteacher. The Amsterdam school suggested that key ingredients for success include:

- close links between school and parents
- regular monitoring of pupils' progress
- a focus on oracy in the early years
- structured and detailed curriculum planning and organisation with a strong emphasis on speaking
- a literacy curriculum focused on subject vocabulary and real understanding
- small teaching groups in the first language to reinforce key learning previously experienced in a second language.

Accordingly, the school decided to focus on oracy for the school's project on bilingual children. Some breadth in the children's learning had to be sacrificed to achieve more depth. Initially, we asked ourselves:

- what do we mean by 'oracy'
- how can we accommodate this work in an overcrowded curriculum?
- how can we monitor what is happening?
- will our assessment practices be useful in our daily work in class?
- will an emphasis on oracy improve achievement?

A book by Pauline Gibbons, *Learning to Learn in a Second Language*, provided a framework for planning for oracy. Gibbons highlights different language functions, and these were matched to the UK National Curriculum requirements and summarised on a planning sheet which was used to shape and monitor longer term curriculum planning.

We ensured that oral and written language learning objectives were included in activities. We identified language structures and phrases to be modelled, taught and practised, and listed the key technical vocabulary which children need to understand and be able to use. Key language structures and some vocabulary were also identified in the pupils' home language so we could reinforce understanding. We realised that a previous emphasis on writing had restricted pupils' opportunities for learning through talk, so we examined our teaching methodology to see how we could raise the standard of children's work through quality talk sessions.

The next stage was to develop more precise and explicit teaching objectives. This involved breaking down more global outcomes into a series of precise objectives. We also needed to make explicit the English structures and key vocabulary that we would model and expect children to use. This required making certain decisions about classroom practice and our role as teachers in presenting/modelling, providing opportunities for practice, exploring meanings and associated meanings and enabling more extensive use of the structures, phrases and vocabulary involved. We now had a basic model for developing oracy in our classrooms, within a lesson format of introduction, main content and summary/conclusion. The model is as follows:

- stimulus or starting point (story, visit, topic, concept)
- focused teaching covering content and language requirements
- independent work by pupils to demonstrate their knowledge, understanding and skills, with support from us
- assessment (ongoing throughout this process) of learning objectives, and linked back to the focused teaching stage
- the use of structured play, making things, carrying out experiments which involve use and practice of the key language learning points
- a performance of some kind by the pupils – in front of the class, or in other ways
- reflection on the performance and sharing of learning outcomes, involving constructive criticism – what can be improved?

The main aim in this process is to move children from understanding procedures to understanding meaning. Instead of pupils being bound by rules and completing set tasks, we want them to be truly independent and able to express their learning in their own words, but using appropriate vocabulary and structures. Internalising these language patterns and vocabulary enables them to apply their learning to new circumstances and situations.

During this process, we pay much attention to assessment against the planned learning outcomes. We combined assessment of 'subject content' with assessment of the language learning. Pupils have to articulate their learning of the subject content through the language learning objectives. With this clearer focus on subject and language learning outcomes we can better assess the extent to which children have reached the objectives, and where they need to improve. Pauline Gibbons' analysis of strategies used by learners when acquiring a second language helped us to work out how to identify the types of language development children need. We were able to identify where children were only capable of using simple and basic language and needed to develop more sophisticated language. Our knowledge has developed into a checklist against which we can make assessments and provide specific support for individual children.

We wanted to integrate the development of English with the use and further development of the children's first language, to help understanding and further language acquisition. We distinguish between concepts which require specific language to express understanding of ideas, and factual knowledge which requires the naming of objects and the use of appropriate vocabulary. Our bilingual teaching and learning policy is based on the need to improve understanding. Our 'bank' of key words and phrases in the children's mother tongues enables us to support children's acquisition of meaning.

The use of the child's first language aids conceptual development. We encourage this dual language approach through involving parents in homework tasks with their children in their home language.

Main characteristics of the AIMS project and what we have learned

- we have a clear understanding, which started life as a hypothesis, that addressing children's oracy and providing numerous opportunities for high quality talk makes a significant impact on children's achievement levels, especially for those who arrive at school with little competence in the main language of the school, the curriculum and the education system in which they are expected to achieve
- we need a planned, structured approach to the development of oracy, based on a clear understanding of the processes of language acquisition and also a sophisticated process of presentation, modelling, reinforcement, practice, performance and review, not simply as a sequence of activities but as inter-related components
- skilled adult users strive for high quality presentation and modelling of language which children can develop and learn to acquire for themselves as a result of the teaching and learning processes involved
- we use a bilingual approach based on a clear understanding of the interrelatedness of the development of two or more languages and where the main languages used are seen as providing opportunities for mutual reinforcement
- we assess against language and subject related learning outcomes and we support individual children's language development based on analyses of these assessments.

Main Outcomes

- as evidenced by inspection and by national test results, children's progress is accelerating and increasing numbers are reaching the national expectation for attainment in English by the time they leave the school; the inspection report describes this as 'a creditable achievement' given that so many pupils are learning English as an additional language

- the pace of progress is accelerating across the school

- children now use more technical vocabulary more accurately and they use English generally more often and more effectively to explain their learning

- children's confidence and competence in using English has increased considerably since the introduction of the AIMS project

- teachers have a greater awareness of language requirements and how they can help children to achieve them; their planning for language development is more sophisticated and better targeted

- teachers are more skilled at analysing pupils' talk and using specific strategies to help them overcome difficulties and refine their language use

- more teachers make selective use of language from the child's first language to support their understanding of English, especially technical language

- overall, thanks to the AIMS project and other factors in the school, pupil attainment at age 7 and age 9 has improved significantly during the life of the project.

Implications for in-service training

- teachers and support staff need training in the theory and practice of language acquisition and need to develop a clear but flexible model of language learning

- training in assessment techniques, analysis of children's language use and in the processes of presenting, modelling, reinforcing, extending and supporting performance of language are essential to children's rapid progress as learners and in acquiring knowledge and understanding

- working together on these issues within a clear conceptual framework at school level is a good method of developing a whole school approach and of sharing expertise and developing it further.

The OFSTED inspection report observed about AIMS:

The school rightly gives the highest priority to teaching spoken English effectively from the earliest stage ... At best, the teaching of English is very good. The teaching of reading and writing is demanding (of the pupils) ... They (the pupils) have moved a considerable way towards closing the gap on national norms and the highest attaining pupils exceed them.

Theme A: Case Study 4

Teaching and learning Danish as an additional language in Odense

City of Odense: Annette Winther
Tel: 00 45 66 148 814 5101
Fax: 00 45 66 140 430
E-mail: KFW@odense.dk
Website: www.odense.dk

Odense has a school population of about 17,000, of whom roughly 15% are of ethnic minority origin. Many children from these families do not speak Danish or have only a weak command of the language on entry to school. Many families have poor economic circumstances. Ensuring that children become competent in Danish as early as possible is a major priority for Odense.

Under Danish law, local authorities have to provide resources to ensure that children who do not have Danish as their first language can acquire it rapidly and effectively. There has been a national project on provision for ethnic minority pupils through which the Danish Education Ministry has made resources available. A report on this overall project is available.

The City of Odense interprets this requirement alongside the parallel requirement under Danish law to provide teaching in a child's mother tongue where the parents of twelve or more children request it. Staff in the city Education and Youth Departments and in schools leading this work are clear that further acquisition of the mother tongue will support the acquisition of Danish and vice versa, especially where children become literate in their mother tongue.

Language development policy in Odense and across Denmark stresses the importance of children being competent speakers and listeners before they learn to read and write. Danish schools do not introduce reading and writing until age 7. So, for children learning Danish as a second or additional language, the focus is on rapid acquisition of oral skills and confidence in listening and speaking in Danish.

Odense regards the teaching of Danish as a second language as a specialist area. It has developed arrangements for initial and in-service training with local and national providers, to provide enough trained staff able to meet the linguistic and wider cultural needs of ethnic minority pupils. So teachers working with potentially bilingual or multilingual children are either trained and qualified as second language teachers or have attended in-service training courses as class teachers. They understand the relationship between mother tongue and second language learning, and the theory and practice of language acquisition.

The basic approach is to create small classes and groups in kindergarten and the first years of primary school where children can be exposed to as much spoken Danish as possible in contexts which support meaning and understanding. Typically, a child might be in a class group of 24 or 25 in a *Folkeskole*; but in any class where there is a significant number of children from ethnic minority backgrounds, an additional teacher is provided so that groups of 12 or 13 can be established. These may be organised in different ways at different times according to the work being undertaken in response to the needs of the children.

At the end of the school day, additional classes in Danish are available to all children whose parents want them. These last for up to two hours.

Aims

- to fulfil agreed policy at city level to resource this area to the levels indicated within a national legal framework
- to ensure that there is training for staff as specialists or developing specialists in this area
- to provide high level specialist support for children learning Danish as a second or additional language
- to ensure teaching groups which are small enough for teachers to interact closely with children as groups and individuals
- to ensure that children achieve competence in Danish as rapidly as possible, and the skills required to develop higher order language skills
- to enable children for whom Danish is a second or additional language to achieve the same levels of educational success as other Danish children.

Danish schools, in common with Scandinavian schools in general, place great emphasis on regular, in-depth consultation with parents about their children's progress. This involves discussions between teacher, parents and child at least three times per year. All three partners are deemed to be equal in this process. Interpreters are used where necessary. This process is an important factor in the educational progress of children and a means of encouraging them to use language for specific purposes and audiences, as well as using increasingly sophisticated language to talk about their progress.

This development is characterised by:

- considerable investment in additional resources per pupil to ensure rapid and deep acquisition of Danish as a second or additional language
- specialist knowledge and understanding on the part of teachers of the processes of language acquisition and development
- considerable attention to developing children's oral language to as high a level as possible in their early years at pre-school and in school
- local policy underpinned by a national framework to ensure that ethnic minority pupils' language needs are addressed
- availability of additional learning opportunities after school
- frequent contact with parents.

What has been learned?

- specialist training of classteachers and language support staff is essential; all teachers catering for the needs of ethnic minority children require initial and in-service training

- investment of resources at an early stage in children's education to ensure that they develop a high level of competence in their second language gets results

- children can and do acquire additional language very rapidly where arrangements and methodologies ensure intensive work in smaller groups and a predominantly oral methodology linked to learning contexts which support meaning and under-standing.

Main outcomes

- children generally make good progress in their acquisition of Danish as a second language

- children's self-esteem and self-confidence are enhanced when they become competent in Danish

- teachers feel that the task of enabling children to acquire Danish rapidly is more realistic when additional resources are deployed especially to reduce the size of teaching groups

- children for whom Danish is a second language progress better in all their learning as a result of developing higher order language skills.

Implications for in-service training

- All teachers or potential teachers of children learning second or additional languages require training in the theory and practice of language acquisition and of the interaction between first and additional languages.

- Training programmes reflecting these requirements need to encompass the cultural and faith background of children.

- These issues need to be addressed to a greater extent in initial teacher training as well as in in-service work.

A video of the work in Odense is available from Annette Winther via the contact information provided above.

Theme B
Teaching and Learning –
Mother Tongues

Why a separate theme?

DIECEC understands from its detailed work and experience that potentially bilingual children will generally become genuinely bilingual – in the sense of being able to operate with a high level of confidence and competence in more than one language – through processes which enable them to develop their languages in parallel and in close connection. DIECEC cities set great store by the interaction and interrelationship between first and subsequent language learning. Children's progress in becoming truly bilingual is greatly enhanced where they are able to use both languages concurrently but in a clear framework which makes explicit where and how, and for what purpose, they are using a particular language.

For example, children progress rapidly when they are encouraged to use their mother tongue to clarify their understanding of a new word or concept in their second or additional language, and vice versa. Because the language of their school and of examinations and qualifications will be their second or additional language, teachers' learning outcomes for their pupils must be directed accordingly, but the mother tongue can vastly aid learning and understanding. This also helps to strengthen and value the mother tongue – an important aim in itself. All this demands consistent and regular interaction between skilled adult users of language and children, especially younger children. For this to happen, additional resources are essential.

Getting the message across clearly to parents

A good and continuing command of the mother tongue is helped enormously by using it at home and in the community and at school by bilingual teachers and other staff. Theme D (Parents as Prime Educators) is important here: parents (of very young potentially bilingual children as well as of older children!) who have not yet mastered the second or additional language should be repeatedly advised to:

> help your child to learn to speak your mother tongue very well; if there are
> fluent speakers of the language among your family or friends, get them to

use it with your child, but make sure this is consistent and within a context and with clues to meaning which help your child to understand. Above all, talk to and with your children, help them to acquire your language; if you are uncertain how to do so, seek help from a local school or the city or education authority. Do all you can to improve your own command of the language of your new home too.

Implementation of policy and practice

Appropriate policy and best practice in mother tongue teaching can be difficult to implement within the financial and human resources available. In some contexts, there could be twelve or more mother tongues spoken in one class and well over one hundred in a city. Making provision outside the home and specifically in school to support all these languages is difficult for schools, education authorities and cities. Finding qualified teachers can be a challenge – but some have solved this by scouring their country for suitable people and training them appropriately. Having enough money to pay the teachers to take children through to formal examinations in their mother tongue is a question of priorities – but it must be a high priority: the evidence about the importance of mother tongue maintenance and development indicates that teaching it will save money later.

Some cities and member states have legislation requiring cities to make provision. This tends to be in contexts where the numbers of ethnic minority children and the number of languages spoken are relatively low, but it signals a clear understanding of the inter-relationship of mother tongue and additional language learning and commitment to fostering it.

We cannot afford to ignore the research evidence. If children's mother tongues are well supported and well taught, and linked to their acquisition of their second or additional language through an extensive common core of content (the school curriculum), they will usually make good progress in both languages and achieve well across the curriculum. There is an important point here – in some contexts, young children can achieve a good level of qualification in an external examination or formal assessment in their mother tongue and this gives them a good start to their acquisition of qualifications and also enhances their self-esteem. These opportunities should not be denied.

DIECEC has identified a number of practical ways in which cities and schools have overcome the difficulties of ensuring good command of the mother tongue and thereby, in the best practice, further development of second or additional languages. These are set out below and illustrate DIECEC's concept of multi-level working: in the most complex cases (for example, schools with many speakers of a wide variety of languages) the answers lie in multi-level solutions involving school, home and community.

- Teaching in as many mother tongues as possible is enabled by extending the school day so that mother-tongue classes can be integrated into overall time-tabling arrangements or added on to the end of school. An integrated approach is preferable since leaving lessons until after school can marginalise community languages.

- Specific, accredited training programmes in language acquisition theory and classroom methodology should be provided for members of ethnic minority communities so that they can achieve a level of qualification and competence to be a teacher or, initially, a tutor or instructor.

- Involve community associations and other organisations in providing mother tongue teaching, based wherever possible in the school the children attend or at their home, so that teaching in and of the mother tongue can be closely related to their school curriculum and using school resources. A good part of the mother tongue teaching should be based on the learning which children are undertaking at school.

- Where supplementary schools are already operating, whether through the initiative of communities or the school, city or education authority, draw these into schools so as to achieve the vital close curriculum and methodological links.

- Emphasise the great advantage of using schools because they have human and material resources which can support the teaching of mother tongues.

- Integrate these arrangements, however funded or provided, with the management systems of the school. Mother tongue teachers need to be seen as part of the school's teaching and learning community and to be valued for their contribution to children's achievement levels and for their wider contribution in helping the school to respond to the cultural backgrounds and needs of particular groups of pupils.

- Integrate the teaching of mother tongues with children's development in their second or additional language. This can be achieved where the mother tongue teacher has fluency in the second language or by deploying a skilled user of the second or additional language alongside the mother tongue teacher.

- Teachers need training to help children who speak the main language of the classroom as a second language to develop their mother tongue through interactions with children who share it and to provide opportunities for children to use their mother tongue to extend and develop their learning. The methodologies involved in this 'bilingual approach' are highly skilled and specialised and require specific training.

Ways forward for schools and cities or education systems

Again, DIECEC does not promote one specific arrangement. DIECEC has found that children do less well at school when the arrangements for mother tongue teaching are divorced from school and curriculum. Close liaison, through multi-level working between the school, community associations, in-service training providers and teacher training institutions is vital and schools and cities must take the lead in securing this co-operation.

Cities which have established arrangements for mother tongue teaching may have to change certain arrangements and practices. In cities and schools where mother tongue teaching is a new or recent need, a multi-level approach is no less necessary and makes the best use of the expertise and enthusiasm of a wide range of people and organisations. Whatever the situation, cities and schools need to have a coherent and cogent rationale for mother tongue teaching, based on the positive outcomes from approaches which:

- place the school curriculum at the core of the content of teaching and learning in the mother tongue
- situate mother tongue teaching as far as possible in schools, supplemented by other opportunities in the community
- specifically link the teaching of the mother tongue with the development of the second or additional language, and vice-versa
- see a good part of mother tongue teaching as an opportunity to reinforce children's existing learning and prepare them for future learning.

Even arrangements based on these principles and using the resources a multi-level approach generates may not be able to cope with the demand for mother tongue teaching. Cities, education systems and schools have to continue to search for ways to teach mother tongues successfully and integrate this with children's learning at school.

Teaching parts of the curriculum in one or more mother tongues is possible in schools which have speakers of only a few mother tongues but becomes difficult where there are speakers of many different languages in the same class. Making provision for particular languages in some schools but not others could interfere with the principle of parental choice; teaching some mother tongues and not others raises questions of equality of opportunity. This highly complex area is best dealt with pragmatically, putting in place the best arrangements possible in the circumstances, within a visible acceptance of the importance of teaching and learning in and through children's mother tongues.

There follows a case study of teaching mother tongues in Odense. This can be considered alongside their teaching of Danish: Case Study 4 of Theme A (p.119).

Theme B: Case Study 1

Supplementary Schools and the teaching and learning of community languages in Bradford

Bradford Education, Steve Howarth, Jani Rashid, Irshad Ahmed
Tel: 00 44 1274 752 315
Fax: 00 44 1274 754 843

Bradford uses the term 'community languages ' to describe 'mother tongues' – languages other than English spoken within Bradford.

Supplementary schools have operated in Bradford for many decades. The Jewish community was running such schools at the beginning of the 19th century. The first Asian supplementary school was established in 1959 by the Muslim Association of Bradford. Since then, there has been a tremendous growth of such organisations providing community language education and religious instruction to children. Almost 80% of the supplementary schools in Bradford are run by the Muslim community, but many other communities – Sikh, Bengali, Hindu, African and Caribbean, Polish, Latvian, Greek, Italian, Ukrainian and Yugoslavian and others also run schools. Demand is great and there are often long waiting lists so some children are taught by parents and relatives in groups at home.

The main role of the supplementary schools which receive financial support from Bradford Education is to provide teaching of a particular community language so that children and young people develop their command of their mother tongue and achieve good levels of literacy. The supplementary schools also provide teaching about the culture and faith of the community of the children and their parents. Increasingly, the schools are linked with or operating within mainstream schools and it is the LEA's policy to encourage and extend this.

A powerful motivation for developing supplementary schools has been the desire of the communities to retain their cultural identity, which is strongly linked to the retention and development of a community language and religious identity. Asian and other parents face the problem of retaining a linguistic identity which will allow all generations of an extended family to communicate with each other while ensuring that the children can operate well in the language of the majority society. Asian parents' enthusiasm for school and their desire for their children to acquire high qualifications have not always been fulfilled so they have set up supplementary schools to ensure that their children retain the cultural, faith and linguistic traditions of their family.

The main educational purpose of a supplementary school is to provide teaching in a community language (for example, Panjabi, Urdu, Bengali, Pushto, Gujerati). Many supplementary schools are held in a study centre attached to a Mosque or temple. Most of these buildings are converted houses. Classes are held mostly on weekday evenings between 16.00 and 19.00 from Monday to Friday and on weekend mornings. The majority of Muslim supplementary schools are open to children seven days a week.

The following table, which is incomplete because of numerous other schools operating on an informal basis, shows the numbers of children attending these forms of supplementary education:

Organisation	Approximate no. of children
Muslim	6,000
Sikh	500
Hindu	300
Italian	40
Ukranian	30
Polish	30
Irish	15
Others	85
Total	7,000

The aims of supplementary schools are:

• to provide teaching and learning facilities for community languages

• to provide facilities for religious instruction in accordance with parents' wishes in an atmosphere which reflects their faith

• to promote the cultural identities of the communities through study of their faith and community language

• to improve communications between parents, children and other relatives in order to preserve cultural and religious traditions

• to support children's self-esteem and emotional stability

• to overcome any socialisation problems experienced by children in a pluralist society.

Supplementary schools usually have their own independent management committee elected by their community. Teachers are generally found from within the community, but it is hard to find sufficient appropriately qualified staff and teaching materials often have to be imported. Staff wages and running costs are often paid out of donations and contributions from the communities and the communities in Bradford have raised several million pounds over the years to support supplementary schools.

Benefits of supplementary education

• children receive a supplementary education in line with what their parents want

• the risk of conflict between parents and their children is diminished due to better understanding of cultural and faith matters

• the community gains self-respect through organising its own self-help initiatives

• there are clear benefits to children's education, including enhancing their self-esteem and self-confidence

- it helps to create better racial harmony by reducing the chances of children being caught between two cultures

- where the supplementary schools are well linked into the provision of formal schooling and vice versa, children's achievement levels in terms recognised by the majority society generally rise.

Difficulties encountered in setting up supplementary schools

- there was an initial hostile reception to the idea of supplementary schools from parts of the majority community. Supplementary schools have had to struggle to gain the support of residents and maintain their right to exist

- raising sufficient money to fund supplementary schools of this type has been a continuing problem for the communities

- most of the buildings purchased for supplementary schooling are not ideal and large sums of money have had to be spent on making sure they meet regulations

- it has not always been easy to find suitably qualified staff.

New developments

- A supplementary schools resources centre has been set up to provide basic resources, advice and guidance and also training facilities for supplementary school teachers and tutors, parents and other members of the community.

- Supplementary schools enter their students for GCSE examinations in community languages. The number of entries is increasing every year mainly due to the excellent results achieved by students entered previously, 79 pupils were entered in 1998. A small number of students followed an A level course – with excellent results.

- The LEA has organised training programmes for supplementary school tutors and teachers. These were arranged to meet the basic training needs of the participants. A more comprehensive training programme is now in place.

- The LEA has a policy statement on supplementary education (available from the contributors to this case study).

Main learning points and outcomes

- supplementary education needs to be linked to the education provided by main-stream schools if the potential benefits of both are to be fully realised

- a strong partnership between schools, parents and community is now being perceived by many as the only way to tackle underachievement

- supplementary schools meet particular needs and give faith communities a sense of fulfilment

- the quality of the teaching and learning at supplementary schools needs to be enhanced through a comprehensive training programme. This can help to ensure much better links between supplementary schools and mainstream schools

- the main issues concern the quality of supplementary schooling and its links with mainstream provision, funding and resources. Many problems could be solved if supplementary schools were physically integrated into mainstrean schools, providing better accommodation and access to resources.

This had implications for **in-service-training**. A comprehensive in-service programme, with suitable accreditation is needed for teachers and tutors operating in supplementary schools. Cities and/or those responsible for the education systems should accept this as part of their responsibility for the provision of training. Furthermore, headteachers and other staff in mainstream schools need training and information about supplementary schooling and its potential for raising of standards in and through schools.

Theme B: Case Study 2

Mother tongue teaching in Odense, Denmark

City of Odense, Annette Winther
Tel: 00 45 66 148 814 5131
Fax: 00 45 66 140 445
Email: annet@odense.dk

The City of Odense has a population of approximately 188,000, of which 7% are from ethnic minority backgrounds; 15% of the school population speak a first language other than Danish, mostly Turkish, Arabic, Vietnamese, Somalian, Serbo-Croat and Urdu. Approximately half the ethnic minority population live in one area of Odense – Vollsmose – and the schools in that area in particular have significant numbers of children and young people for whom Danish is a second or additional language.

Mother-tongue teaching must be provided by Danish schools as soon as there is a demand from the parents of twelve children for this to happen in a particular language. The provision must be made from the start of statutory schooling at age 6. Additional funding has to be provided by the City for this and there is a legal requirement to provide three lessons a week.

The lessons must be given by a native speaker, employed by the headteacher of the school concerned. In some instances it is difficult to employ qualified teachers and in others there are some doubts about the teachers' qualifications. Lessons generally place at the end of the school day or later in the afternoon.

Pupils are offered mother tongue teaching for the nine years of statutory schooling and this is taken up by 57% of the pupils who could access it, not all of whom attend for the full nine years. Attendance is voluntary and depends on the wishes of the parents and the pupils.

That there is legal requirement in Denmark to provide mother tongue teaching in all languages for which there is sufficient demand demonstrates that the importance of mother tongue teaching is recognised, for reasons which include its contribution to the effective learning of Danish as a second or additional language. Because the teaching takes place in schools, it provides access to resources and allows for good links between the teaching of the mother tongue and of Danish as a second or additional language. The teachers of mother tongues are not necessarily qualified to teach other subjects.

Main outcomes

- pupils enjoy speaking their own language freely and having the opportunity to improve their command
- the cultural and linguistic links between the pupils and their close and extended family are secured by this provision, reducing the risk of children being caught between two cultures and being unsure about their identity
- they are able to use their mother tongue to clarify concepts and understand more clearly what they are being taught in Danish at school
- many – though not all – parents appreciate the value of the provision of the mother tongue classes and understand its importance.

Implications for in-service training

- mother tongue teachers need training in methodology and the theory and practice of language acquisition
- often they also need an induction programme about the Danish school system and the requirements placed on teachers in terms of planning, classroom practice and evaluation
- some teachers who have spent a long time in Denmark may not be as confident in their use of the mother tongue as some pupils; they need opportunities to ensure that their own command is adequate
- some teachers of mother tongues do not speak Danish, and this limits the extent to which they are able to help pupils to understand the curriculum they are being taught at school
- in response to some of these issues, there is an annual one week training programme to enable them to extend their qualifications and knowledge of the Danish system. They can also apply to attend any training course offered to other teachers, although this can be difficult as these courses often clash with times when they are teaching. Considerable local support is provided through meetings with an adviser and the development of networks of mother tongue teachers.

Theme C
Improving Basic Skills –
literacy, numeracy and information
and communications technology

DIECEC advocates that competence in the basic skills of literacy, numeracy and Information and Communications Technology (ICT) is a fundamental human right. All children and young people, regardless of their background, should be able to acquire these basic skills because they are so fundamental to other learning and to the very processes of learning. Children should acquire these skills to threshold levels at an early stage and then be able to increase their competence progressively and consistently as they grow older. Their centrality to higher levels of achievement throughout the curriculum is well proven. For many ethnic minority and socially disadvantaged children there is also an important question about access and the gap between their levels of achievement and those of other groups: failure to acquire good skills in these three basic areas will only increase this achievement gap.

Yet far too many young people and adults have inadequate basic skills. Precise statistics are not available but a great many, possibly up to 50% in some cities, of 11 year olds lack adequate basic skills. Children from ethnic minority backgrounds are usually over-represented in this group, as are children who live in areas of multiple disadvantage in the cities. Many adults, too, have weak basic skills, are functionally illiterate, far from numerate and have had little or no opportunity to develop ICT skills.

These situations require multi-level measures. Improving children's basic skills at school is far more difficult if there is little or no reinforcement of the need for them at home or in the community. As the case studies, principles and policy measures exemplified below illustrate, multi-level actions do work. They can produce quite startling results when applied consistently and intensively across a school or a community.

Literacy
It is worth repeating the message from Themes A and B about the inter-relationship of literacy in the mother tongue and literacy in the second or additional language. Schemes which promote and develop literacy in mother

tongues must have their place alongside measures to improve literacy in the child's new language. We also need to consider the debate in Theme A about when formal literacy skills are best introduced.

For example, what does 'reading at home' mean for a young potentially bilingual child? It means reading books in both languages, including separate and dual language books – but at what point? What about the availability of books in mother tongues, or the cases where there is no formal written form of the oral language? Many non-European languages (and some European languages!) place great store on the oral tradition of story-telling, so there are few written stories.

Where children are learning a second language, they need first to engage with text in the form of short simple stories based on pictures as soon as they can. Suitable help at home will certainly be helpful. But research suggests that in the households of certain linguistic minorities reading with children has not been a tradition.

Consequently, education systems and schools need to engage with parents, families and communities to develop the concept of parents and others as reading partners with children, and see this as a key part of their role as the prime educators of their children. In immigrant families this will generally be more difficult to achieve (in terms of reading stories and other texts in the second language). But the difficulties for subsequent generations should not be overlooked, especially where one parent is recently arrived and does not speak or understand the second language – yet! All parents can nonetheless enjoy books with children, whether they read them in their first, second or both languages or just glean the story from the pictures. Arrangements which develop the tradition of reading at home by giving parents the skills they need to do this are likely to benefit children's progress.

Schools and education systems cannot assume that parents of ethnic minority or indeed other children will read with their children, pursue activities which help to develop literacy (for example, play language-based games) at home or understand how to do these things when they recognise its value. Schools, the education authority, providers of further and adult education, local community organisations and other voluntary bodies need to work together to promote the importance of such activity at home and within the communities, and provide programmes of training and information to help parents and others to support children's acquisition of literacy. Accreditation and certification of these programmes seems to increase their attractiveness to parents – for some, it may be the first time they have received a recognition of their achievements.

Schools need to ensure that ethnic minority children become literate as soon as they are able, but with regard for the dangers indicated in Theme A – beware requiring children to develop literacy skills before they are ready. Literacy skills are not acquired by osmosis! They have to be taught, and children have to practise them in contexts which help with other aspects of their education. Schools must devote much time to literacy and structure their preparation for and teaching of it so that children progress. Some education systems are putting in place specific arrangements for teaching literacy and numeracy, and these are described in the Case Studies. Some cities have designed imaginative and successful schemes for developing parents' abilities to support their children's reading and language skills and in some instances numeracy and these too are noted in the Case Studies.

Some of these approaches have developed into Family Literacy and Family Learning Schemes, where adults and children in a family learn together at home and sometimes in other contexts. DIECEC strongly endorses these approaches, partly because they correspond to the concept of learning at home as well as at school and in the community, but mostly because they enable fathers and other males to become involved in learning and also provide good role models for children. Boys may be held back because they see learning and education through their experience at school and home as a predominantly female undertaking, especially at primary level.

Numeracy

Many of the points made here about literacy apply equally to numeracy. By numeracy DIECEC means children's and young people's competence and confidence in using and understanding operations based on the four rules of numbers – addition, subtraction, multiplication and division – and being able to solve problems and undertake number operations. Numeracy includes a range of practical skills which are needed not just in mathematics but in other areas of the curriculum and, crucially, in practical situations beyond school.

Schemes similar to those introduced to ensure competence in literacy have been introduced for numeracy also, including projects which involve and engage parents so that children's competence in numeracy can be reinforced and extended at home and in their community.

There is a specific issue for second and additional language learners here: numeracy and mathematics in general requires using and understanding technical language in precise ways; it involves thought processes which depend on 'internal language processes' – using language in the mind to solve problems and work out number-based operations. Second language learners have to be given the skills to use the technical language of mathematics in this way and to understand, for example, that the same concept or operation (subtraction) can be expressed in a variety of ways: 'take away', 'subtract', 'being less than', 'difference between' etc. but also that there is a correct technical term (subtraction).

As with literacy, a multi-level approach is needed for numeracy; schools, in partnership with other organisations, need to work with parents so that basic number rules and concepts are reinforced and further developed at home.

Information and Communications Technology (ICT)

DIECEC sees ICT as a wide range of basic skills of increasing importance to learners in general and to children and young people from ethnic minority backgrounds in particular. Evidence shows that ICT is an important tool for learning, that it has motivational potential and that its use for learning, accessing knowledge and communications purposes will keep growing.

At the same time, DIECEC believes that good education is largely a social process, involving interactions between teachers and learners, and that ICT cannot and should not replace this. However, as a tool for learning, a potential accelerator and reinforcer of learning, and a significant aid to learning for children with communication and other difficulties, ICT has enormous potential.

Multi-level approaches are again important. Many children who already achieve well can extend their learning even further through using ICT at home and at other points in addition to school; the challenge to education systems and schools is to make ICT available to children, young people and adults who cannot afford their own facility (although with the development of new learning systems, fibre-optic and other networks and reductions in the costs of hardware and software, basic access may become more affordable) through the co-ordination and opening-up of resources, public access points and other mechanisms which make access to ICT more realistic for more people.

Schools themselves can play an important role in this by opening up their facilities to pupils and parents outside normal school hours. Many schools now do this, and find that it evokes multiple benefit in terms of motivation, competence, self-esteem and general learning. One of the DIECEC Projects – Réussite Scolaire (Success at School) – has specifically focused on the role of multimedia technology in supporting the learning of very disadvantaged pupils, with considerable success.

An increasing number of software packages are available to schools in the different cities and member states, which can and do help with acquiring skills in ICT itself, and in literacy and numeracy. The role of ICT in reinforcing and improving competence in the other basic skills is a factor which schools should use in their overall strategy for improving literacy and numeracy, but not at the expense of interaction between teachers and learners.

Resources to support basic skills

Resources are often available but they are fragmented. For example, resources to support literacy developments may be available from:

> the national and local education system
> a national agency with responsibility for basic skills amongst the adult population
> local authorities, including the city
> further and adult education providers
> local or national funding designed to finance regeneration schemes in deprived areas
> European funding for education, regeneration, or social welfare projects
> local or national trusts or charities
> other voluntary bodies
> training agencies and providers.....

.....you can probably name others! The problem is that too often, these funding regimes and the initiatives which they support each operates in isolation. This is where cities and education systems have to move in. They are in a unique position to co-ordinate resources and support and promote coherent approaches which scaffold literacy and other basic skills developments across a whole community. Schools can do this too, but they have fewer flexible personnel resources and less flexible time; also, an individual school acting in isolation, no matter how effective it is with its school population, cannot affect a whole community or area. Clusters or families of schools working together can, but they usually need the support of their city or education system to do so.

So the Case Studies which follow concentrate on multi-level approaches which involve the co-ordination of measures and funding across a whole system, community or city. One attraction of working on basic skills as a priority is that it is relatively easy to achieve results quickly, to measure baselines and chart progress. Suitable, short assessments of reading, number and ICT competence exist in most contexts, and the process of analysis and identification of further measures needed is also relatively simple once the outcomes of these assessments have been analysed.

If children are denied the 'human factor' in learning, especially in basic skills, they will not perform at their best. A visit to one school revealed a child working through page after page of numerical exercises without contact with a teacher.

He was working with 'paper and pencil' but could equally have been working on a computer. He had successfully completed about twenty operations before his book revealed a series of apparently random errors. When questioned about this he replied 'You only get the teacher's attention if you make a mistake'. At least he had cracked the system!

Theme C: Case Study 1

Literacy in Bradford: the Better Reading Partnership

Bradford, Steve Howarth, Liz Fisher
Tel: 00 44 1274 751 257
Fax: 00 44 1274 484 362

Bradford has a school population of about 83,000, of whom roughly 28,000 are of South Asian origin, mainly from Pakistan, India and Bangladesh. Many children from these families speak little or no English on entry to school. Many families have poor economic circumstances and live in sub-standard housing. Educational achievement levels have generally been low, although some children with a good overall scaffolding for their education succeeded academically, and increasing numbers of pupils who start statutory schooling with little or no English are achieving at national expectations by the age of 7 or 11 – the stages of national assessment.

Reading and literacy have been a particular priority for Bradford LEA and many of its schools, and developments such as the Better Reading Partnership have made a significant contribution to the rising standards. Since 1995/96 the Education Committee has had a policy in Bradford to prioritise language and literacy development generally. At the same time, an agreed policy on teaching reading was developed. This involves the use of a variety of methods according to the needs and current reading behaviours of children but it is based firmly on the notion that children need to be taught reading skills and that reading for understanding is a fundamental skill.

There has been a commitment to partnership with other people and organisations in pursuing the aim of better literacy for all. This involves volunteers and adults other than teachers supporting children and schools, backed up by teachers and LEA staff with considerable expertise in how to teach reading. The approaches to teaching reading reflect those developed by Marie Clay and the Reading Recovery Programme, initially in New Zealand.

The Better Reading Partnership trains adults other than teachers to be reading partners for children who are at the average of their class in reading attainment. The children are aged from 6-13. The adults follow a specialised training programme which is accredited, so they receive recognition of their achievement in becoming a 'reading partner', which is good for their self-esteem.

The training is practical and challenging. It uses a one-way screen behind which a child is reading with a trained partner. After the initial training, in which the reading activities are observed for two days, the reading partners receive further support and advice from a trained teacher at the school they go to work in. Each reading partner then works with a child for three fifteen minute sessions each week for ten weeks. The approach is very effective with children learning English as their second or additional language. The reading partner records the child's reading behaviour and progress. A range of books suited to the stage of reading development and age of the children is available.

In each session, children start by reading a book with which they are familiar and can already read well, followed by one they have started to read and through which they can make further progress, followed by a new book which the reading partner selects and introduces to them. The reading partner always ensures that the child has understood the meaning of what she or he is reading, using a variety of techniques.

As a result of this intervention the children make rapid progress with their reading and can make an average gain of six months in reading age after the 10 week input – more than twice the normal rate of progress. Further evaluations of their reading skills and levels indicate that they continue to maintain their good progress after that.

This approach is **multi-level** in that it involves:

- a city initiative derived from an analysis of city-wide data about reading levels; it is funded by a partnership of the city, a government organisation, the local Training and Enterprise Council (TEC) and schools

- pupils, teachers, parents, volunteers from businesses and other adults work in partnership. It provides accreditation of competences for adults, many of whom have no formal educational qualifications

- it addresses reading in the contexts of school, the home and community

- it is evaluated at individual pupil, class, school and city levels.

This development is characterised by:
- a multi-level approach to the training of adults other than teachers; some are identified through a national charity, Volunteer Reading Help

- a highly successful programme in which schools and volunteers want to be involved

- a scheme which builds the self-esteem of adults and children and enhances self-confidence

- the improvement in reading levels and increased levels of self-esteem raise the children's achievement levels across the curriculum.

What has been learned?
- narrow approaches to the teaching of reading (for example, seeing the teaching of phonics as the main or only way of teaching all children) will cause some children to fail as readers and in other aspects of learning

- each child's reading behaviour has to be analysed in order to determine, on an on-going basis, the most appropriate next step for their progress

- adults who are qualified teachers can be effectively trained in a short time to become reading partners

- the nature of the training and the fact that it is accredited have a positive impact on unqualified adults' self-esteem and their own learning

- multi-level approaches involving a range of partners and people working at different levels have many benefits, not just for the children and their achievement but also for the adults and organisations involved

- focusing on children's reading skills affects achievement levels generally and can help to bridge any existing gap between levels of girls and boys.

Main outcomes

- Children involved in the Better Reading Partnership make gains of between 150% and 250% on their previous reading score as measured by standardised tests of reading age

- this acceleration of progress continues after the ten-week intervention. For many, this unlocks a major key to the whole curriculum

- there are positive effects on children's self-esteem and their contacts with their peer group, and on parental support for them and their school

- the interactions between the reading partners and the children improve the children's abilities to express themselves and, specifically, to talk about books

- there are positive outcomes for the reading partners in terms of self-esteem and confidence; for some it is the first time they have had an educational achievement recognised

- schools benefit from the involvement of the reading partners in a wide range of ways

- the scheme is replicable in many different ways and areas; for example, Bradford is developing a similar scheme aimed at improving children's spoken language.

Implications for in-service training

- some teachers need additional training in the teaching of reading, especially if they have been trained in one approach only (for example, phonics)

- there is immense benefit in training volunteers, adults other than teachers and older pupils (from 16 upwards) to be 'reading partners'; and having a specific methodology which has been proved effective makes this unintimidating and rewarding

- these reading partners need support from a trained teacher in the school

- cities need to create a training resource to meet these needs; minimally, it should consist of two trainers who work well together and the facility of a 'one-way' screen.

Children, staff and other people involved in the Better Reading Partnership had this to say:

'I found the Better Reading course to be very enjoyable. It was very informative without being too technical. I felt relaxed and able to absorb information in an informal setting. I have gained valuable skills which I can implement in my reading partnerships and also in ordinary school life.'

'I have really enjoyed being a Better Reading Partner. I enjoy being with children and getting feedback, knowing that I am doing something good.'

'The Better Reading scheme is a great asset to the school...I think I have learned a great deal and hope to apply the knowledge I have gained in helping children with their reading. The records we keep (Running Records etc.) are very helpful in accessing the level the child is at.'

'I like working with Mrs. Cussans because she helps me do a lot of reading.'

'Mrs. Hirst helps me with my reading. I like reading lots of books with her.'

(The last two from Asian children.)

A video and booklet about the Better Reading Partnership are available via the fax number indicated.

Theme C: Case Study 2

Primary numeracy centres and the UK national numeracy strategy

Birmingham, Suraj Masson, Brian Wardle
Tel: 00 44 121 303 8080
Fax: 00 44 121 303 1196

In 1995, the UK Government announced a pilot project to improve numeracy skills in primary schools. Called The National Primary Numeracy Project, it involved thirteen Numeracy Centres based in Local Education Authorities. Birmingham and Bradford LEAs each developed one of these centres. Within the Numeracy Projects, the cities particularly emphasised the need to address the numeracy skills of ethnic minority children and the language issues arising from the need to acquire the technical language of mathematics. This theme has been taken up at a national level by the Primary Numeracy Project. It is a vital theme because evidence shows that many pupils for whom English is a second or additional language perform less well than they should in mathematics generally and in numeracy in particular, not because they do not understand the mathematics but because they do not have the language skills to enable them to respond accurately or develop their understanding and ability to reason.

The UK government, Birmingham and Bradford Local Education Authorities (LEAs) and schools agree that improving basic skills is an important part of the overall strategy for raising the achievement levels of ethnic minority and educationally disadvantaged pupils. The pilot Primary Numeracy Centres opened in 1996. In 1998 the UK government announced a National Numeracy Strategy involving all primary schools, to secure improvements in the numeracy skills of children.

In some instances, Primary Numeracy Centres have paid particular attention to working with parents so that they can better support their children's acquisition and reinforcement of numeracy skills.

The aims of the Primary Numeracy Project are:

- to improve levels of numeracy in all schools, including pupils learning English as their second language

- to ensure that a structured hour of numeracy teaching and learning is undertaken every day for every class throughout primary schools

- to raise the profile of numeracy as a vital basic skill in the eyes of parents and the wider public

- to set and meet national, LEA and individual school targets for improvements in numeracy.

Each LEA appoints two or more numeracy consultants who are trained in the requirements of the National Numeracy Strategy. These consultants then work with schools to

- undertake an 'audit' (analysis and evaluation) of their current provision for numeracy, diagnosing relative strengths and weaknesses

- agree an action plan with the school to develop its strengths and address any weaknesses; this action plan includes agreed targets for competence in numeracy skills at the ages of 7 and 11 with interim 'milestone' targets

- train two key staff from the school, one of whom must be a senior teacher, in the requirements of the numeracy project

- support these two key teachers in training their colleagues so that the numeracy hour is implemented consistently throughout the school.

Schools monitor their progress in implementing their action plan, with a major focus on the extent to which they are achieving the targets. The targets are the subject of an agreement between the Governing Body of the school and the LEA, which can intervene if it feels the targets are being set too low.

The National Numeracy Strategy is based on successful work in the pilot projects and other developments which have resulted in children achieving higher levels of numeracy. Its basis is as follows:

- a specific approach which involves giving teachers the skills to address pupils' numeracy development needs using a wide range of appropriate strategies; there is a particular emphasis on mental agility and the ability to carry out number operations 'in their heads'
- teaching and learning specific skills in numeracy, focused on the 'numeracy hour'
- raising expectations of the levels of competence which all children can achieve
- an approach which reflects a view of teaching and learning based on Vygotsky's theory of learning. There is an implication in the strategy that using this approach will have a broader, positive effect on teaching and learning within the school.

This development was characteristised by:
- a structured and prescribed approach to improving standards of numeracy in schools
- a common approach across all schools based on a clear theory of teaching and learning
- auditing and target-setting at individual school levels
- clear accountabilities of LEAs and schools to meet their targets.

So what has been learned overall as a result of this development? It is too early to evaluate the impact of the National Numeracy Strategy on a wide scale, but the pilot projects are producing favourable outcomes even though they only been running for a short time before the introduction of the national strategy. There is no reason why children who speak English as a second language should not progress at the same rate as those who speak it as a first language. This work has also shown that structured approach to teaching numeracy generally has a positive effect on pupils' skills and motivation.

(*The main outcomes can be found on an electronic file requested from Birmingham*)

Implications for in-service training
- Teachers and support staff in schools need training in structuring their work on numeracy with particular emphasis on the linguistic demands of the curriculum
- the model of working with two key staff as in-school 'experts' who provide training and support for other staff appears to be effective for any whole school development
- headteachers and other staff in schools often need training in the processes of audit, identification of strengths and weaknesses, target setting and evaluation.

Theme D
Engaging Parents as Prime Educators of their Children

Introduction

DIECEC believes that parents' role as the prime educators of their children needs to be promoted and supported by national and local education systems and by cities and schools, working with already established parents' organisations. This theme should be a priority for every city, education system or school seriously concerned with raising achievement, whether or not this is specific to ethnic minority children.

To accept that children do not learn only at school is not to excuse schools or to shift responsibility from schools to parents. Children and young people nearly always achieve well where parents form one side of the educational support triangle of school, home and community. The potential role of all parents in providing this support is indicated by the evidence of where it is actually happening.

Educational systems, teachers and parents have to deal with ever-increasing expectations and curriculum demands. Many parents, even those who did well at school, find it difficult to keep up with changes in the education system and the work expected of their children at school. Parents who had negative experiences of education find it even more difficult. Some can feel – and become – marginalised in their children's education. DIECEC is concerned to identify ways in which parents can be better engaged with and by schools, so as to support their children's learning.

Emphasising rights and responsibilities

The tendency in many member states to open up education systems to market forces and emphasise the accountability of schools to parents has been counterproductive. While accepting that schools and education systems must be accountable and produce results, DIECEC notes with concern a trend for parents to see themselves as having little role in educating their children. Many believe that if they deliver their children to the school door, they are entitled to expect that they will emerge well educated. So parents feel unsure about how to help their children, or feel 'de-skilled' because education has changed so much and has a new and impenetrable jargon.

When positively engaged by schools, parents and family members can play a vital role in supporting their children's education – significant enough for DIECEC to identify them as the prime educators. The huge majority of parents have knowledge and skills, understandings and attitudes which can help children to learn. Ethnic minority children with extended families have an even broader potential source of learning.

Refugee and orphaned children, traumatised children and those who experience family breakdown or cannot rely on a supportive framework at home will need special arrangements for support. Cities and systems need to work closely with the services and agencies which organise or undertake such surrogate arrangements so that they are able to operate in loco parentis.

The balance between parental rights and responsibilities is a key issue. DIECEC sees many instances in which parents are insufficiently engaged by their children's school but also many parents who appear uninterested and are reticent to approach the school (except when there is a problem). But many schools are working closely and effectively with parents and thus making life better for their teachers (and the parents!). It is true of all these schools that the pupils do better because of their parents' involvement in their education.

Interrupted education

This theme affords the appropriate context for discussion about 'interrupted education', particularly about extended visits by families to their country of origin during school time. These extended visits usually last from three weeks to eight or nine months and are more common among some communities than others. Along with other factors (apart from illness) which can interrupt children's education for a considerable period, they need to be addressed consistently.

DIECEC recognises the value of such visits. They represent important cultural and family experiences for children and young people. Visiting another country is often acknowledged as a significant educational experience, so why should these visits be any different? Comparisons between the ways of life, traditions and cultures of the two countries provide genuine potential for learning.

But long visits will generally arrest progress and achievement in the children's formal schooling, effects which may last longer than the visit itself. Younger children especially may take some time to readjust to school. They will have missed not just specific learning opportunities and chunks of curriculum content but also chances to extend their learning skills and capacities. There are instances in the DIECEC cities of children going on extended leave of absence just when they are mastering their second language, and backsliding significantly. Going abroad just before examinations is equally damaging for young people, just when what they have learned over a period of years is about to be brought together, reinforced and checked out.

Cities and schools need to draw these issues to the attention of parents through meetings and other direct contact or through discussions at a mosque or community centre. Written documents are more useful for ease of reference and to ensure that a balanced view is maintained but they do not replace the discussions. The problem for increasing numbers of schools is that because they are held accountable for the achievement levels of all their pupils, extended leave of absence will affect their performance records.

Cities and schools can do a certain amount to mitigate the effects of extended absence, assembling study packs and using open and distance learning techniques so children can undertake school-related work while they are away. Work with parents exemplified in this theme can help to ensure that the children's education will continue during their time away. There is some good practice but such arrangements are normally no more than damage limitation.

DIECEC's concern is that ethnic minority pupils in schools in the cities should achieve at levels which are at least equal those of other children, and extended absence works against this. Cities and schools must recognise the value of such visits but work with parents to minimise their negative effects, for instance by travelling at the least disruptive times for their children's educational progress. Such visits should be negotiated between parents and school, not simply accepted as a fact of life. DIECEC does not believe that schools should remove children from their roll unless it is clear that they will not return, as this exacerbates the problem for them on their return. Accordingly, cities should establish clear guidelines for their schools on this issue, covering

- the length of absence regarded as acceptable; DIECEC suggests a maximum of three weeks of school time

- the desirability of ensuring that longer absence overlaps with school holidays (bearing in mind the climate of the country to be visited and the costs of fares at different times)

- the need for parents to ensure, with the school's help, that their children's education and, wherever possible, the development of their second or additional language, is treated as a priority while they are away

- the need to avoid key periods of the academic year, for example during statutory assessment or examinations or when especially important work is being undertaken

- the need for parents to prioritise their children's education and to realise that extended absence will almost certainly impair their achievement levels in the short and possibly the longer term.

Experience in DIECEC cities shows that where these issues are tackled with parents and the guidelines implemented in a consistent fashion, the length and frequency of extended absence decreases and achievement levels tend to rise.

Involving parents as a key to raising achievement

Engaging parents and promoting their role is crucial to raising achievement. It is important not to blame parents for appearing not to support education, nor to patronise them, nor to under or over-estimate their starting point. The DIECEC cities take great heart from a common realisation: virtually every parent wants their children to do well, and this is especially true of parents from ethnic minorities. Many of them realise the value of education but relatively few fully understand the educational system or know how to use it or how to support their children's learning. Yet we know that parents can often make positive contributions to schools and their children's education. They bring valuable skills, knowledge and understanding about not just their own children but as parents, adults and perhaps as volunteers, employers or employees in a different sector of activity. They also bring views, to which schools must try to respond, about the need for the school to reflect their cultural, faith and linguistic backgrounds.

It is worth repeating that children achieve well when they go to a good school and where their parents support their education and have, or have been provided with, the skills and knowledge to do so in practical ways. Schools which can select their pupils may well do so on the basis of parents' ability and commitment to supporting their children, because they know that these children are likely to attend school regularly, work well and achieve good results.

A curriculum for working with parents

It is not enough to generalise about 'working with parents'. DIECEC cities have come to realise that there are several aspects to this theme, including:

- promoting with parents their role as prime educators in ways which convince them that they will be supported in fulfilling it
- providing information in their first languages about the school system and how it operates – for example, what are parents' rights and responsibilities; what are the usual expectations of pupils at different ages; how much homework should 14 year-olds be doing?
- educating parents so as to improve their own educational levels and employability but also to enhance their ability to support their children's education

- developing specific skills in parents from the outset so that they can support their children's education at home and in the community
- liaison between individual schools and home – communication and mutual understanding helps the school to respond effectively to children's needs and parents' expectations
- effective arrangements for reviewing children's and young people's progress with parents; these processes may lead to home/school agreements
- directly involving parents in school life in positive and practical ways.

The DIECEC cities have found that there is a progression in this curriculum for working with parents. Many parents need to develop their role as the prime educators of their children and schools – especially secondary schools – have to be more open towards parents and make themselves welcoming places. Cities, schools and other providers are responsible for providing solid scaffolding for parents who want to help their children but do not know how to, or who have themselves experienced poor education and shy away from or even reject schooling for their children and further education and training for themselves.

Engaging parents – a multi-level approach
Co-ordination at city or neighbourhood level

A multi-level approach is essential to involving parents in schools. Many organisations and services provide some help, support or educational opportunities for parents and other adults but in many cities these initiatives are uncoordinated. One essential feature of effective work is therefore to put in place from existing human resources a co-ordinating mechanism at city or neighbourhood level for the work undertaken with parents by schools, further and adult education organisations, training agencies, voluntary groups and self-help groups of parents. Each city needs to decide on the nature of this mechanism, but the DIECEC Network has found that it has to be there and it must include people who are themselves parents. In the most effective models, one particular service or organisation has responsibility for this co-ordination role as well as providing some practical support for parents. The service responsible, supported by the political and professional leadership of educational and other services, can work with others, including the schools and parents themselves, in engaging parents more effectively with their children's education, especially the parents who seem most reluctant. This service can also provide schools (who must be responsible for the work with their parents overall) with a framework of partners who can actively help in engaging and working with parents.

Experience in the DIECEC cities shows that partnership working is the most effective way of engaging parents. The schools definitely cannot work alone. The partners who can be involved include:

- the schools themselves

- the city's or education system's service for co-ordinating work with parents (or the service with the potential to do so)

- providers of further and adult education

- parents' associations and organisations, including ethnic minority organisations

- other voluntary groups which work with particular groups of parents or provide training and support

- local training agencies and providers

- cultural mediation services

Cultural mediators or home/school liaison staff are vital to this framework. It is essential to establish effective contact with parents, for example, with fathers who traditionally do not see a role for themselves in the early education of their children; or with women from cultures which encourage women to be home-based. The issues are thrown into sharpest relief by parents who are new to the city or who have little or no personal experience of education – and whose initial priorities are to do with living accommodation, employment and making ends meet.

The case studies below show how cultural mediators or home/school liaison staff are a consistent feature of cities' and schools' efforts to establish and maintain effective contact and to broaden this out to programmes which cover the 'curriculum for parents' set out above. These staff must have the linguistic and inter-cultural skills to gain the confidence of the families and so are likely to be recruited from the communities themselves. Raising achievement often depends on their being enough skilled staff to ensure the involvement of parents. Why? Because...

... a number of the case studies provide evidence that working effectively with parents can have as great an impact on achievement in a school which is performing at a reasonable level as can internal school improvement. Achievement levels at one school rose from well below to above national expectations of 11 year-olds over a four year period, during which the school concentrated its efforts on parental education and involvement. This is not an exceptional. Working with parents is a vital part of any effective school improvement strategy.

Involving parents through arrangements for evaluation or consultation

All the schools studied make arrangements for direct contact with parents through what are called evaluation or consultation sessions about their children's progress. Arrangements for (and attendance at!) these meetings vary considerably. In the best practice observed by DIECEC, these meetings are highly valued for their contribution to children's and young people's progress. The teachers are given time to prepare their meetings with each family. Information is sent to each home in advance, together with questions about each area of the curriculum that parents are asked to discuss with their children, and the children are specifically prepared for this by their teachers.

Parents, teachers and children are accorded equal status in the meetings. Each meeting ends with targets being agreed and the contribution of the three partners set down in the form of an agreement. The meetings are held on a termly basis and are taken seriously by all concerned. If ethnic minority parents want an interpreter one is provided.

The diverse arrangements for consultation demonstrate the different extents to which parents are engaged in this one aspect of working with them. DIECEC observes that there is still much work to be done within this theme. DIECEC cities agree that effective education depends on a good partnership between home, school and education-related support services. Working with parents so that they are in a position to exercise their responsibilities as well as their rights is a key theme in raising achievement, and may be a starting point for schools which have already improved their teaching and other internal processes but have yet to see any significant improvement in achievement levels.

Theme D: Case Study I

SOWA – a support agency for parents and ethnic minority children and young people in Antwerp

Antwerp, SOWA, Maja Christiaens
Tel: ** 32 3 234 98 40
Fax: ** 32 3 234 98 39

Antwerp has a significant and growing population of people from ethnic minority backgrounds. As in other DIECEC cities, there are major issues about the achievement levels of children and young people and about the ways in which their parents are able to support their education and training. Many young people see success at school as one way of escaping from the downward spiral of deprivation. SOWA's mission is to help these young people to turn the tide, by directly or indirectly supporting them. Especially with younger children, we target the parents and support them in their role as parents who can participate in their children's education.

Many of the parents of ethnic minority pupils do not have a good command of Dutch and lack literacy skills. So their understanding of the school system, their children's progress and other factors which affect achievement levels is often inadequate.

SOWA was established in 1992 by the Alderman for Education in Antwerp, to work with parents so that they can better support their children's education. It was recognised that underachieving pupils' learning needs to be supported at home and in the community as well as at school. At first work was focused on schools, parents, children and young people in the state education system. Now that ethnic minority pupils have entered the Catholic and Regional systems, SOWA has become involved there too, so it now works across the three elements of the overall education system in Antwerp.

The school is the starting point for SOWA and it works with parents on the situation of their children at school. Parents can ask SOWA directly for support, as well as participating in the activities it organizes.

SOWA has an overview of work with the parents of ethnic minority pupils and is in a position to co-ordinate developments. It has developed many community-focused activities. With schools acting as the hub, a network of contacts and support is being developed among the parents themselves, between the parents and schools, and the local community organisations which in turn support the parents. As a result of this networking, there are consultations and discussions at several levels:

- at municipal level, within the framework of the city's equal opportunities policy. Projects supported by the city and run by SOWA can be related closely to the needs of the target groups. Alternatively, the projects can be related to and co-ordinated with each other – for example, close links are established between the programmes for teaching Dutch as a second language, reception of new arrivals and anti-discrimination projects

- with the three administrative authorities for the education system (State, Regional and Catholic School Boards), with some projects being organised across the system and others made specific to the situation of each type of school

- with members of local communities who can express their needs and work with SOWA to develop projects which can address them

- with other organisations including schools, voluntary and local community organisations, parents and young people.

The multi-level approach adopted by SOWA thus includes a wide range of partners who help to support parents in their role in their children's education and who co-ordinate projects which work at different levels – individual pupil and parent, schools and teachers, education authorities, community organisations etc.

At the time of this case study SOWA employed 34 staff, about 50% of them from ethnic minority backgrounds, as community workers/cultural mediators. SOWA's activities are closely linked and inter-related and embrace language and literacy projects for the mothers of ethnic minority children, the 'Performing Arts' project and school/ community links and network development.

SOWA organises language and initial literacy lessons in Dutch and in Turkish as well as Dutch language courses for literate migrant mothers. 200 mothers in fifteen groups across four primary schools are taking courses. Five specialist teachers with expertise in teaching Dutch as a second language were appointed for this programme.

The Performing Arts project organises project weeks in schools, often on multicultural themes. Activities include drama, circus arts, Djombe etc. The aim of the workshops is less to teach techniques than to develop processes of working with children and parents from different backgrounds, with the team of facilitators acting as role models. This team has a core of four people and is joined by others for particular activities.

The school/community links and network development work is mainly undertaken by the sixteen school/community workers, mostly appointed from the ethnic minority communities. They start school/community projects in each school, each of them working closely with about five schools. The content of these community projects varies greatly. They include key activities such as mediation and conflict resolution, organising mother groups for learning and support, learning activities for parents about the educational system and aspects of the school curriculum establishing school councils, pedagogical advice, stimulating leisure and recreational activities amongst parents, children and young people at school or elsewhere, advising school staff in relation to cultural issues. The projects always focus on particular target groups and involve them in their design and implementation. They work closely with the school over each project, ensuring that its staff understand how it can help them to develop their work with their diverse school population. In each project, the school/community links worker plays a significant role and is the first point of contact for the parents.

The school/community links workers also provide cultural mediation at the request of the school in resolving issues affecting individual or groups of pupils and parents. The workers are close to the target group and advise from that position on how the school can take into account the needs and expectations of the parents. They also mediate during parent consultation/evaluation meetings about issues in school or individual pupils' progress. They make extensive home visits and telephone contacts to maintain and develop contact with the parents and to provide a fixed contact point and support. Home visits help mothers who do not leave the home or visit the school.

One aim of the school/community activities is to ensure long-term support by developing networks. As part of this, social contacts between parents and self-help groups are encouraged. The mother groups are characterised by informal meetings for mothers at the school, to break down barriers and promote mutual understanding through joint activities. Wherever possible, local community organisations are involved in the organisation of the mother groups so that mothers can help one another. Wide-ranging questions are discussed about education and their role as educators of their children. Exchanges of experience help to build the self-confidence of the women and create lasting bonds between them so that they can support one another in the future.

The mother groups stimulated a need to develop a more structured approach to providing information. The school/community workers have developed different forms of training and education for the parents on a wide variety of topics (for example, swimming lessons for Muslim children, going on the annual school outings, what the children learn in certain subjects).

The workers support and advise parents in all these activities. Parents approach SOWA with questions and issues they wish to raise, and SOWA helps the school to respond. The workers can, however, also work with the parents without directly involving the school.

This development is characterised by:

- being a community-based organisation that operates a comprehensive approach to working with parents, providing information, tackling issues and helping schools to respond to an increasingly diverse pupil population

- a multi-level approach which impacts at different levels and multi-agency working, with a particular emphasis on involving local community organisations and empowering ethnic minority communities to support themselves and organise activities

- a specific focus on educating parents to support their children's education and improve their own skills

- work with mothers on issues which might otherwise cause ethnic minority children to be excluded from certain activities

- clear working arrangements with the schools – for example, a separate contract is drawn up with each school for each of SOWA's activities

- projects that are organised with and by the target groups

- the clear objective of helping ethnic minority people and communities to attain positions where they can help themselves and depend less on outside support.

What has been learned?

- parents really are concerned about their children's education and want them to achieve as well as they can but their concern is not always expressed in ways which teachers understand and many teachers do not realise that the parents are interested and concerned

- effective change rarely comes about if you work only with one party in a process which involves many. So a multi-level approach is essential and schools in particular need to recognise that they cannot provide effective education without involving other partners, especially parents

- an organisation like SOWA cannot operate in isolation from other organisations and needs to work closely with a wide range of partners. The development of SOWA coincided with developments in the education system designed to meet the needs of ethnic minority pupils more effectively. It is important to co-ordinate these developments.

Main outcomes

- Parents now find it easier to come into school: they feel better informed about what the school is trying to achieve, and how. They are more able to support their child's education, and they know who to consult about the issues.

- The parents and their needs and backgrounds are better understood in the schools, especially by teachers. Teachers now contact the parents more spontaneously about matters of daily routine and more important issues. For their part, the parents recognise when a school is seeking to respond to them and appreciate it.

- Many ethnic minority parents, especially mothers, have benefited in a range of ways from the activities in which they are involved, with positive effects on their self-esteem and confidence, basic skills and understanding of the school system.

- As a result, many more pupils understand that their parents can help them and that they can be well supported at home as well as at school.

Implications for in-service training

- SOWA staff and the staff of similar organisations need training in areas such as: their own 'deep' command of the second language; how to involve and engage members of the target group in projects and activities; intercultural communication; working with a range of partners.

- City staff and other staff working with parents need training in cultural backgrounds and on how to win the confidence of ethnic minority women. They need to know how to observe and respect cultural norms and traditions.

- Staff working with parents need to appreciate their baseline in terms of knowledge, understanding and previous educational experience. What parents can achieve or the degree of support they can provide for their children should not be underestimated.

- At policy and structure level within cities, training is needed in terms of effective structures and forms of organisation which can be set up to co-ordinate a comprehensive programme of training and support for parents of ethnic minority children. In many cities there is considerable activity in this area, but it is insufficiently coordinated.

Theme D: Case Study 2

Cooperation with parents in Lakkegata and Vahl schools

Headteachers: Geir Johansen (Lakkegata) and Trine Hauger (Vahl)
Lakkegata
Tel: ** 47 22 197 180
Fax: ** 47 22 687 763

Vahl
Tel: ** 47 22 578 110
Fax: ** 47 22 578 119

Vahl and Lakkegata are both inner city schools in the eastern part of Oslo, and both have exceptionally high percentages of ethnic minority pupils. For example, in Lakkegata (a primary school with three classes in each grade from 1st to 7th grade), about 85% of the 450 pupils do not speak Norwegian as their first language. The fact that the majority of our pupils speak languages other than Norwegian as their first language means that we have to be conscious of language needs and demands for the teaching of all subjects and aspects of the curriculum. The children on each level are divided into teams and this makes it easier to organise the teaching for groups of pupils at approximately the same stage of language learning.

The teachers' educational background is varied in terms of both training and previous experience. Some are specialised in pre-school teaching; some are bilingual in the main community languages, Panjabi-Urdu and Bengali.

The two schools are near each other and are very similar in terms of pupil population and socio-economic background. Both have faced great challenges in pursuing their aims of greater parental participation and involvement so have readily co-operated in projects intended to meet these aims.

Children's lives and adults' lives are inextricably linked – children are dependent on adults and the conditions they provide. Since adults have a strong effect upon children's lives and learning, an important aspect of the work of the two schools has been to strengthen and support the role of adults in their children's education. The project is based on the assumption that joint activities, information and communication are all important for co-operation. Consequently, the schools try to make room for forms of co-operation in which adults and children to do things together. These shared experiences provide a starting point for the parents and schools to gather information about each other, and this in turn enables them to talk about important aspects of children's lives and their learning.

As a school we must recognise that co-operation projects mainly take place within the surroundings of the school. Our aim should be to increase parents' school-related competences, which will help them to participate with confidence and understanding in various school situations. The school should inform and communicate in a way which recognises that each party involved has an equally valid role in pupils' learning and development. Open and welcoming schools enable parents to find out what goes on there, by observing and participating in school activities. Schools have to stop being institutions which in some ways compete with families over issues of socialisation and their children's learning, and become places which include parents and their cultures far more actively.

Aims of the multi-level work

- to involve parents in ways which help their children to make better progress in their education

- to improve children's ability to complete their statutory education successfully

- to develop a positive climate for collaboration between the school, parents and children

- to develop this climate through joint activities, information and genuine communication

- to provide parents with opportunities for observation and participation in school activities

- to build awareness and skills amongst teachers in school/parental co-operation.

The project emphasises measures which foster communication between the school and parents about their child's progress and the involvement in their respective class. By trying out new approaches we hope to increase parents' interest in the school's curriculum and their influence upon it. The range of measures to be covered includes:

- enabling access to the legal framework for education and national education plans through education and training courses, discussion evenings on certain issues and seminars for parents

- involving parents in the work of the schools and their teachers by holding extended school-days with open classrooms; co-ordinated bilingual programmes for parents and pupils working together; holding open days for parents and pupils; and by transfering appropriate powers to parents

- establishing a library and computer room and renovating an old part of the building to provide a place for parents to meet, to help develop skills and the understanding of different cultures.

One development which has been implemented and evaluated is the 'Welcoming' days. Children and their parents are usually expectant but apprehensive when the children are about to start a new school. Initially, hope and optimism prevail among the pupils, parents and teachers. We want to use this climate of optimism to present ourselves and our school in a way that fosters confidence and trust. We do this through a three day programme for parents, children and teachers just before the school closes for the summer, where we try to create an atmosphere in which parents feel free to take part in their children's school activities. We try to demonstrate our methods and explain them clearly, and to make room for dialogue. Our main objective is to establish co-operation between pupils, parents and teachers so that the children develop feelings of pride in their parents and trust in the school. We also try to create an atmosphere which confirms parents in their parental role as important educators of their children and supports them as participants in their children's daily school activities. We try to give parents the opportunity to ask for and receive information through observation, participation and communication. We try to explain the school's work with new children (6 year-olds) clearly and to enable all participants in the welcoming days to experience various forms of co-operation. We are concerned to develop an awareness amongst teachers of the importance of a good shared basis for co-operation between parents and school.

The key words associated with our welcoming days are 'play and friendship'. We demonstrate our work through social interplay, games, pre-literacy activities and language development, avoiding activities that demand fluent Norwegian.

This development is characterised by:

- a planned programme of induction aimed at engaging parents in supporting their children's education at school

- a programme based on a clear understanding of the value of parental participation, understanding and support

- providing information and opportunities to participate in educational activities and understand why the school does certain things and how the parents can help to support these approaches

- creating opportunities for parents, children and teachers to learn with and from one another by working and playing together

- involving interpreters for parents who have little or no Norwegian.

What has been learned from the 'welcoming days'?

- they conveyed to the parents that the school wished to be open towards them and to help them to support their children's education

- they are excellent opportunities for communication about the school, individual children etc

- it is important to explain the school's pedagogical approach to parents and to enable them to participate in a sample of activities

- parents respond positively to this sort of opportunity to become involved with their children's education

- effective dialogue is possible when teachers, parents and pupils participate together in a well thought out programme.

Main outcomes

Pupils: the children were able to establish the basis for good social and working relationships. Teachers got to know their names and every child became acquainted with another or several other children. According to the parents, the children enjoyed the experience, made new friends and were now really looking forward to starting school in August.

Parents: the parents appreciated the opportunity for their children to get to know the school and make some friends before school actually started. They enjoyed being involved in the programme and were grateful for the opportunity. An atmosphere of openness towards the parents was achieved and the parents felt better informed about the school's ways of working and also about how they could help their children.

Teachers: the teachers who participated in the welcoming days all felt that it was a good move to include parents in the process of learning. Teachers in one school felt that preparation time and time for reflection on the question of home/school co-operation had been too short but teachers in the other felt that the preparations had produced many ideas about parental participation. Both schools followed the same pattern of preparation, so the difference in reaction appears to be due to the fact that most of the teachers in one school were very experienced whereas most of the staff of the other were new and some had just qualified – so the preparation was new to them. The schools are developing a programme of educational counselling and advice for parents, adding to the programme initiated by the welcoming days.

Implications for in-service training

- the rationale for and practical implications of genuine parental participation need to be clear to all concerned

- in-service training needs to create a clear commitment to parental participation based on evidence of its value in terms of the children's educational success

- teachers need to be given opportunities to consider the importance of parents' roles as prime educators of their children and the inspiration, professional stimulation and opportunities for creativity in developing these roles

- there is a need to work on a consistent, planned basis with parents in order to achieve a high level of understanding of the education system and processes used by schools, and to enable them to support their children's education and development effectively at home

- the school needs to have an internal dialogue about its attitude towards parents and the ways in which it presents itself to them.

Theme E
Additional Opportunities for Learning

Note: this theme is also partly considered in the introductions and case studies for Sections 2 and 3 – Multi-Level Working in Cities and Whole Education Systems, and Multi-Level Working in Schools. The roles of cities and schools set out in those sections of the Handbook underpin the comments here about the scaffolding of children's and young people's education, and their contributions to the provision of additional opportunities for learning.

The need for additional opportunities for learning

Many children and young people from ethnic minority backgrounds have high levels of support at home and from their extended family. And many have additional learning opportunities, for example, classes or activities at weekends and in the evenings organised within their community to develop their first language, enhance their education or learn more about their faith and cultural background. The extent to which these activities support and complement their work at school (and vice versa) varies. Where there is a good level of complementarity, children often achieve well. However, for some children from ethnic minority and educationally disadvantaged backgrounds, school may be virtually the only place where they have access to positive learning opportunities. It therefore makes sense to look at additional opportunities for learning and how they can be developed and made accessible to them.

DIECEC has a broad view of the concept of achievement. The different aspects of achievement (academic, personal, social, cultural and so on) complement and depend on each other. If pupils' experiences outside the classroom mean they are not ready for learning within it, they are unlikely to be able to take full advantage of their schooling. This theme looks at how cities, schools and other services, agencies and voluntary bodies can work together to provide a wide range of educational, recreational and leisure opportunities for children and young people in and outside school hours, and during school holidays. These activities should certainly have their own aims – enjoyment among them – but the more they reinforce learning at school, the better the chances of success in educational terms for the children and young people involved.

That children need effective scaffolding for their education outside as well as inside school is part of the rationale for this theme – as analysis of the range of opportunities for learning accessed by children who achieve at high levels proves. They usually have good facilities for doing homework and further study and ready access to libraries and computer facilities outside school. And they may be involved in a range of other activities which reflect particular interests (the arts, sport, hobbies etc.) or enable them to sample activities they have not tried before. Most of this will be organised for them by their parents or their school and many of the activities will contribute in some way to their achievements in school.

This is part of the effective scaffolding which academically successful children often have at their disposal and is often, but not always, related to social class and economic prosperity. The challenge for the DIECEC cities, schools and education systems is to make this scaffolding available to and accessed by all children and particularly to underachieving children or children who have specific educational needs.

Additional learning opportunities potentially include the following benefits:

* reinforcement and extension of learning undertaken at school

* opportunities to learn in different ways, which can help learning at school

* opportunities to succeed in activities not done at school and which raise their self-esteem

* opportunities to learn alongside adults other than teachers

* through a combination of these factors, opportunities to improve their levels of motivation, self-esteem and achievement at school

Cities and schools need to be aware of many issues when implementing a comprehensive programme of additional learning opporunities: safety is an obvious one, as is, specifically, child protection. It cannot be assumed that the providers of activities will operate in ways which will respond to the backgrounds and needs of the children. A brief analysis of most cities reveals that a good range of opportunities is often available and the issues are less about funding and more about co-ordination, availability and access, and about the nature of certain activities. The Handbook does not go into all of these issues in depth, but a brief consideration of access issues will be helpful.

Access to Additional Opportunities for Learning

DIECEC has observed many different traditions and cultural differences related to additional learning opportunities. Some cultures have a tradition of undertaking community-based or other activities which support and extend people's learning and these tend to be introduced to children at an early age and the school system, implicitly or explicitly, assumes that they are there and being accessed. Access is not normally a problem for those who have been brought up in this tradition, but the very strength of the tradition and its often monocultural and excluding nature shuts out people of different cultures.

The traditional activities of some cultures relate closely to faith background and to the importance attached to family and extended family links. Although not directly related to the education system, such traditions provide strong support for personal and social development, often within a strong religious context. Again, access is easy for those within the tradition, but the time involved may restrict children's and young people's access to other, more school-related learning opportunities.

In other instances, the nature of activities is determined by more basic factors – including survival. Education and learning tend to be relegated to a lower level of priority than basic needs – like food and shelter.

This is a simplistic and incomplete analysis; the point is that the existence of a range of activities does not mean that people will access them. DIECEC's experience suggests that the following are some of the crucial factors and features of the provision which determine the level of access of ethnic minority children, young people and adults:

- local availability – that is, within safe walking distance

- cost, especially in areas of high unemployment

- the balance of people from different cultures attending the venue – it must be in a place which ethnic minority people consider appropriate and in which they can feel comfortable

- the timing of the activity: for parents, evenings are often inconvenient; for children, early evenings are often spent at mosque or supplementary school. Weekends and daytime are usually better

- the cultural norms demonstrated by the venue and the tutor for the activity – staff involved in providing these programmes need to be from the community themselves or, at least, interculturally skilled

- availability of childcare facilities and the level of confidence and trust in the providers.

Cities, schools or whoever is providing or brokering the activities cannot rely on 'traditional' methods of advertising their availability. Information printed in community languages can help although more direct means of communication are found to work best. Planting messages with key people in a community is best. Talking to local religious leaders, community leaders and people who have good contacts with a local community and using local community radio stations will often prove more effective than the most splendid printed material.

Interest and enjoyment

Successful practice in this theme illustrates an important feature of effective learning: we all learn more effectively when we have a real interest in the activity, can participate actively, enjoy it and have some 'stake' in it. Above and beyond the issues of availability and access to activities and the fine examples of provision and co-ordination provided by the cities stands the issue of how children can be involved in the design of activities – not just out of school, of course, but also especially where the curriculum and teaching methods are increasingly prescribed by national authorities. If schools have to conform to national requirements and so have to restrict the opportunities for children and young people to determine or at least be involved in the design of activities, it may be better to adopt different approaches to activities organised by schools and others outside the formal curriculum and outside school hours.

The range and co-ordination of additional opportunities

Before proceeding to the case studies for this theme, it is worth listing some activities cities can put in place themselves or help schools to set up with their local partners:

- playgroups, crèches and activity centres for very young children, including parental workshops about early child development

- pre- and after school clubs which provide child-care, food and education-related activities

- study support centres and homework clubs, staffed by good role models

- specific revision programmes before examinations

- recreational and educational programmes during evenings, weekends and holidays (cf. the 'Partner School' concept below)

- computer clubs (for learning and entertainment) and cybercafes

- co-ordinated programmes of cultural, sporting and recreational activities for people of all ages

- specific educational support programmes which help to improve basic skills

- summer and holiday schemes or programmes which incorporate some or all of the above ...and so on.

Who are the '**local partners**' with whom the city should co-operate in a co-ordinating role so as to put this educational scaffolding in place? Although the partners will vary from city to city, they will include:

*   schools themselves, as the 'hub' of educational opportunities in their community

*   parents and other adults in the local community

*   services such as youth and community and leisure and recreation, whether these are provided by the city or another organisation

*   further and higher education services

*   other providers of adult education

*   training agencies and training providers

*   voluntary groups and associations, including community associations

*   cultural, sporting and other associations or clubs

*   religious centres

*   libraries, museums and galleries

In DIECEC's experience, if cities do not co-ordinate the work of these partners and activities, no other body will! Without co-ordination, provision will be patchy and incoherent. It will lead to over-provision in some areas and of some types of activity, and under-provision in others. Cities have to play their part in securing an effective support system for learning outside school hours.

Cities and schools have a particular responsibility to work together to seek to ensure the availability of as many relevant learning opportunities as possible for their children, young people and parents. It is, on the basis of all the evidence available to DIECEC, entirely in their interests to do so: their particular roles, and how they can fulfil them, are suggested in Sections 2 and 3 of the Handbook. DIECEC's evidence is that the achievement levels of children and young people depend to a considerable extent not just on attending a good schools but also on the range and suitability of their additional opportunities for learning. As part of the evidence for this DIECEC cites, on the positive side:

*   the examples of schools which have significantly raised the achievement levels of ethnic minority pupils by working in this way

*   the positive effects of specific activities such as homework clubs, study support centres and pre-examination revision classes on the achievement levels of young people

- the achievement levels of some ethnic minority children and young people from communities which have recognised the value of additional learning opportunities

- the levels of demand and take-up for such activities from ethnic minority families

- the positive effects on achievement levels of supplementary schooling, where this is closely linked to the curriculum of the local schools...

and on the negative side:

- the considerable evidence of regression in children's achievement levels as a result of long summer holidays or other lengthy absence from school during which they have little or no access to structured learning opportunities

- the numbers of children from ethnic minority backgrounds who under-achieve even though they attend schools which have been judged to be good or very good

- the concern expressed by schools about the low levels of first-hand experiences available to some younger children from certain ethnic minority backgrounds

- the sporadic but increasing outbreaks of rioting in some European cities amongst ethnic minority youngsters, often attributed at least in part by they themselves to inadequate opportunities to engage in productive activities in their spare time.

For all these reasons, DIECEC considers this theme to be another key factor in raising the achievement levels of all children and young people, not just of those from ethnic minority backgrounds. The case studies below illustrate some of the different ways that DIECEC cities have successfully approached their role in providing and co-ordinating such opportunities.

Theme E: Case Study 1

Birmingham's University of the First Age

Birmingham City Council: Suraj Masson, Maggie Farrar
Tel: 00 121 3030 2606
Fax: 00 121 303 2505
E-Mail: mfarrar@lea.birmigham.gov.uk

Birmingham is a large, multicultural city with several areas of multiple disadvantage. The city believes that children and young people need opportunities for learning outside school but which contribute to their education and progress as learners. The University of the First Age has been established to provide such opportunities for children aged 11-16.

(Further context information about Birmingham is on p.87)

The University of the First Age (UFA) provides additional learning opportunities for children and young people outside the normal school day. It uses a range of sites including schools, community settings, Higher Education Institutions, Further Education Colleges and Arts Centres. Young people can access the learning experiences by registering at their school or at a local community centre. The UFA makes no charge to young people and receives substantial support in both cash and kind from a range of partners across the city. Its work is underpinned by Professor Howard Gardner's Multiple Intelligence Theory. Birmingham also organises a Children's University for younger children along similar lines.

Aims of the University of the First Age

* to extend learning beyond the mainstream school environment
* to use accelerated learning techniques drawing on some of the latest research into how the brain works to 'lift the lid' off learning
* to involve a range of people in the learning experience – teachers, older students, parents, members of the local community and business volunteers
* to contribute to the process of raising achievement levels in Birmingham
* to provide enjoyment and motivation
* to develop new approaches to learning which can affect teaching and learning in schools
* to respond to the theory and practice of response to multiple intelligences by focusing activities on different approaches to and contexts for learning.

Young people who are involved in the UFA can choose to take part in a variety of activities, which are interest-led and usually intensive. They will have the opportunity to extend learning beyond the school curriculum while at the same time extending their literacy, numeracy, communication, thinking and information technology skills. Recent learning experiences offered to young people include:

- accelerated literacy and numeracy

- maths, music and dance programme

- glass technology

- philosophy for children

- accelerated Spanish in one week

- transportation problem-solving in the city of Birmingham

- small vehicle design and manufacture at the University of Central England.

The Young People's Parliament project forms part of the work of the UFA. This encourages young people to take up the role of young citizen and to interact with young people locally, nationally and internationally, through email and video-conferencing. Recent events include the young people's general election conference in 1997 and the shadow G8 summit in Birmingham in 1998.

This development is characteristised by:

- a multi-level approach to providing additional educational opportunities involving co-operation between teachers, young people, parents, businesses and the local community

- access for children to a wide range of activities which enable them to engage in learning activities during the 85% of time they spend in the 'home and community' curriculum

- developing different approaches to learning which aim to improve young people's motivation to learn and to develop their self-confidence as learners.

Main learning points and outcomes

The UFA was launched in 1996 so is still in its infancy. It is a partner in the national evaluation project of Study Support in partnership with the Prince's Trust (which funds after-school study support and homework centres) and Strathclyde University. Birmingham University is also a partner in the local evaluation of the UFA. The main findings of these evaluation processes so far indicate that:

- young people are eager to engage in learning in their own time

- the brain is a powerful learning tool and accelerated learning approaches which utilise a significant amount of the brain's potential can have a marked effect on young people's achievement

- the local community and parents have a powerful role to play in a learning how to work in partnership with teachers

- learning out of school hours, in different contexts and with a range of different people, can significantly enhance self-esteem and confidence.

Implications for in-service training:

The insights gained into effective learning with young people can be transferred to an adult learning context. Teachers and the young people themselves hugely underestimate their learning potential. Accelerated learning strategies have much to offer the teacher training environment and teachers' own personal learning as well as their actions in classrooms. So the learning gained through the UFA has relevance to initial and in-service training and to teaching and learning strategies used in schools.

What children, staff and other people involved in the Project or development work have said:

'Usually things fall out of my head – but here they stick'

'I like to learn while moving around – it helps me to remember more'

'I like learning in different ways – it makes me see that I am smarter than I thought'

'How could I ever go back to teaching in the same way again?' (tutor)

'I don't know what you've done – but keep doing it!' (parent)

A video made by students of the first UFA summer school is available, as well as numerous documents and copies of materials.

Theme E: Case Study 2

Additional opportunities for learning through the Rising Youth School and the '*Fritidsbutik*' (Leisure-time Shop)

City of Odense, Denmark. Kirsten Wandall Annette Winther, Claus Voetmann (Rising Ungdomskole – Municipal Youth School)
Tel: ** 45 66 12 15 86
Fax: ** 45 66 13 49 80
E-mail: riusk@image.dk

The City of Odense has a population of about 189,000 of which 7% are from ethnic minority backgrounds. The main ethnic minority groups are Palestinians, Turks, Moroccans, Vietnamese, Somalis, Iraqis and Iranians. The presence of ethnic minority groups in the city is relatively recent.

There is a tradition in Denmark of Danish people participating in a variety of community-based activities. This starts from an early age and Danish children are used to being involved in additional activities outside school. This case study describes some of the activities available in Odense and ways in which ethnic minority pupils are encouraged and enabled to access them.

The Rising Ungdomsskole (Youth School) is a non-compulsory municipal youth school which provides a range of educational and recreational activities. The school has around

850 students and club members, about 30% of whom are from ethnic minorities. The school serves two very different districts in the same area of the city, one relatively prosperous with low-rise housing and a very deprived area, Vollsmose, with a population of 12,000 living in one square kilometre in high-rise concrete blocks. This area has a very poor infrastructure.

Aims of the Rising Ungdomsskole

*   to provide a range of additional educational and recreational activities, especially for educationally disadvantaged young people

*   to provide activities and assist with the welfare of newly-arrived young people and those who are at risk

*   to organise and run projects which develop particular provision, especially introductory education for newcomers

*   to put in place a holistic approach towards children and young people and their families by working within a multi-level approach.

The following activities are example of the work of the Ungdomsskole:

*   leisure-time educational courses in the afternoons, evenings and holidays which complement statutory education. Activities include foreign languages, mathematics, design, teenage culture, white-water rafting, trekking. Any legal activity is possible!

*   clubs for younger (10-14) and older (14-18) year-olds, running normal youth activities combined with ideas generated by the young people and from the Management Board, which includes parents

*   the activities of the 'Project Division'. These are funded by the municipal authority and provide introductory education (language teaching, including Danish as a second language), citizenship and an introduction to Danish democratic processes and opportunities to engage with the other activities of the school. The school has about 70 young people involved in these activities, representing thirteen different nationalities and all between 17 and 22 years of age. There is close co-operation with the social welfare authorities responsible for the newcomers and for refugees

*   for some students, the work of the Project Division represents a first opportunity to learn Danish and understand Danish society and culture in order to make the transition from initial language training to admission to the normal further and adult education system; for others, the provision represents a 'second chance'

*   the Rising Ungdomsskole is in charge of the 'Fritidsbutik'. This is an information and advice centre in the centre of Vollsmose. The Fritidsbutik draws together information from an extensive range of providers (public, private, voluntary) about the activities they provide and makes this available to young people so they can find out about all the opportunities.

This development is characteristised by:

- a specific school designed to offer a wide range of additional learning opportunities and also co-ordinate those provided by other services and organisations

- a holistic approach to the education and recreation of young people, involving social welfare and care as well as educational opportunities

- specific provision for newly-arrived young people to help them to come to terms with life in Odense

- second chance opportunities for students who have not succeeded in the Danish school system

- regard for the cultural and faith backgrounds of the ethnic minority students

- teaching methodologies which reflect the variety of activities available. The staff of the school are trained and experienced in working with young people and sensitive to the needs of newcomers and young people from different cultural backgrounds.

Theme F
Promoting intercultural Understanding and Combating Racism

This theme is about intercultural education in its most straightforward definition: how to work with children and young people to help them to acquire attitudes to diversity and difference which result in their demonstrating and, in their own ways, promoting a positive view of diversity and people from other cultural, faith and linguistic backgrounds. Simple to say, but very difficult to achieve because

- many children and young people will be subject to powerful and frequent blatantly racist opinions, especially out of school, and these views may well influence them more than those of adults and their school peers with whom they spend only about 17% of their time.

- open and covert racism, including institutionalised racism, are still the norm rather than the exception in many places and contexts

- peer opinions and pressures in this area are very powerful, and part of the dominant peer culture may be racist

- it is often seen to be more exciting, credible and 'cool' to provoke and harass than to develop positive relationships with people from different backgrounds.

The DIECEC cities have discovered that the development of effective anti-racist measures has to be a truly multi-level undertaking. In one dimension, these levels cover peer and adult role models and attitudes; in another, they involve the formal and the hidden curriculum in schools; in another, they involve different agencies and services working effectively together and reinforcing positive messages; and in yet another, they include the provision of effective guidelines and sanctions applicable to racist behaviour.

One thing is clear: overt and covert racism has to be challenged and refuted at every turn. Cities and schools have a major responsibility for this, as do national governments, agencies such as sports and cultural associations, formal antiracist and other equal rights-based organisations and institutions such as the European Commission, which took a lead through the European Year Against Racism (1997) and the 'One Human Race' media campaign. We focus here on two main areas: specific measures to challenge and combat racism and racial harassment, and educational processes which promote and develop positive attitudes to diversity and to racial and religious harmony among children, young people and adults.

The roles of schools and cities

DIECEC is clear that schools, cities and education systems have to stand up and be counted on this issue. They have to promote the richness and value of diversity on the one hand, and work to eradicate racism on the other. The DIECEC cities and their schools often have powerful policy statements, backed up by specific measures and practices. A key question for schools and cities to consider is the balance they achieve between processes and procedures for dealing with racism when it arises and measures which promote the value of diversity and actively reject racism.

Schools and cities need to present a strong example through their policies and practices, the ways their staff relate to each other and to children and young people, and the composition of their staff. The people and groups whom children and young people admire and seek to emulate, especially cultural icons like rock stars, television personalities or sports people can be engaged nationally and locally to provide positive messages about diversity. Schools and cities have an important role in engaging such people for this purpose.

A further successful approach is to emphasise similarities rather than differences. Taking the example of different world religions, the fact that they are underpinned by many of the same basic values may be obscured by stressing the different ways in which beliefs are observed. Children who learn by example that differences are a reason for fear or disrespect will probably develop a xenophobic value system, whereas children who learn that differences are a source of learning, excitement and interest, and that similarities are generally stronger than differences are more likely to develop a positive view of diversity. The curriculum of schools and its delivery are therefore major vehicles for combating xenophobia and racism.

Prevention is better than cure, so developing positive attitudes to diversity through education is important. But how can cities and schools affect the extent to which children and young people encounter strong and consistent racist messages which influence them and may defy reasoned argument? DIECEC's response is predictable: one important feature of effectively scaffolding children's and young people's education outside as well as inside school is that this should include consistently positive messages about diversity and strong rejection of racism and xenophobia.

Additional learning opportunities such as those represented in Theme E are one part of this scaffolding. Many cities involve their museums, galleries and other public exhibition centres in offering exciting and interesting glimpses of the art, culture and traditions of different peoples from around the world and these exhibitions are promoted in schools.

Local media should be involved in asserting the value of diversity and condemning racist attitudes. Cities and schools should form working relationships with the local press, radio and television services to ensure this. Some representations by the media should operate at a subliminal level but they should also overtly reject racism and promote the value of diversity.

This theme places an important responsibility on cities and schools, together with their other partners who contribute to the scaffolding of learning, to ensure that their staff tackle and reject racism wherever it occurs and promote positive views of diversity. All organisations involved with children and young people need to provide training which will enable staff to respond appropriately.

DIECEC would like to sound a warning about the nature of some of the procedures set down for employees of cities, other local authorities and organisations in relation to racist behaviour or harassment. DIECEC understands and indeed promotes the need for such guidelines and procedures, but doubts the effectiveness of those that are unnecessarily cumbersome and involve much time and effort. Direct approaches, similar to those increasingly used to combat bullying, appear to be most effective. These confront the perpetrators with the consequences of their actions and, at an appropriate time, bring them face to face with their victim and strong sanctions are enforced. Recording instances of racist behaviour is important; DIECEC suspects that many instances go unreported because of the labyrinthine nature of some of the procedures involved. As the case studies below indicate, there are innumerable ways to affirm diversity and combat racism.

Theme F: Case Study 1

The Interfaith Centre (IEC)

Bradford LEA: David Jackson and Julia Kendall
Tel: 00 44 1274 731 674
Fax: 00 44 1274 731 621
E-mail: interfaith@legend.co.uk
Website: www.bradford.gov.uk/education/interfaith

Of Bradford's school population of about 82,000, about 28,000 are of South Asian origin, predominantly from Pakistan, India and Bangladesh, and most actively practise their faith. Four of the six major world religions – Christianity, Hinduism, Islam and Sikhism – are well represented, with very significant numbers of practising Muslims.

The Interfaith Education Centre (IEC)

The Interfaith Education Centre provides advice, resources and other practical support to schools and other organisations about world religions. It helps Bradford LEA to fulfil its statutory responsibilities for Religious Education in schools by developing a locally agreed syllabus which reflects the faith backgrounds of pupils in schools. The work of the Centre is regularly reviewed and updated in consultation with representatives of the four faiths mentioned above and of Buddhism and Judaism. It has strong links with the different faith communities of Bradford and emphasises the commonality of values and beliefs which underpin different faiths. It provides information and also a forum for the discussion of issues affecting the different faith communities of the District.

Aims of the Interfaith Education Centre

- it is City Council policy to establish, maintain and develop an Interfaith Education Centre which helps to assure good relationships between different faith communities

- UK national policy requires local authorities to develop policies and syllabuses for religious education which reflect the faith backgrounds in the area; this has been achieved in Bradford through the IEC

- the IEC aims to work proactively with schools and organising specific support for the teaching of religious education, citizenship and values education.

The Centre works through schools and colleges and with pupils, students, and teachers, and community and faith organisations, and with health authorities and the police, city services and national organisations. It has established effective local, national and European networks. Staff are drawn from local Christian, Hindu, Muslim and Sikh communities and are responsible for arranging and leading visits to places of worship in the city, and making visits to local schools.

This IEC is characteristised by:

- a multi-level approach to teaching and learning about major world religions in which the identity and characteristics of different faiths are retained and valued whilst emphasising the commonality of basic values

- being both proactive and reactive. It provides practical advice and training for schools and other organisations to assist with intercultural issues, helping to maintain for example, good relationships between people of different faith backgrounds during the Gulf War

- active involvement in European project work for three years, leading a project on interfaith education and helping to raise the profile of teaching and learning about world religions at the levels of the European Commission, cities and other education authorities, and in schools.

Main outcomes and learning points

- links between the work of the IEC and levels of achievement are indirect, but the work of the Centre contributes significantly to pupils' self-esteem, their feelings of identity and their readiness to learn

- teachers benefit from the training and resources provided by the IEC and from its work in promoting better understanding between the faith communities

- although attitudes towards people of different faith backgrounds are largely unproblematic, the IEC provides a forum for discussing any concerns that arise

- schools report that the input of the IEC enhances the culture of the school and the self-esteem of the pupils whose faith and culture are now more valued. In particular the programme of providing separate faith worship for Christian, Hindu, Muslim and Sikh pupils in 52 schools has contributed greatly to developing a positive ethos and a climate

- The IEC aims to support and encourage multi-level schools, seeing them as the hub of education in a community, enabling home, school and community to function together. Schools which cater well for ethnic minorities and for diversity in general, encourage, enable and co-ordinate community provision either in or outside of school. The IEC sees the task of the school as to work with the community to promote the openness and accessibility of the school and to persuade people to participate in local education initiatives designed benefit the pupils.

Implications for in-service training

- staff not just in schools but in mainline city services, the police, health authorities and youth services as well as voluntary organisations require training on the cultural backgrounds and religious traditions of people from different ethnic groups

- people from the communities themselves are best suited to provide this training, supported by the well-resourced IEC

- the existence of the IEC is a constant reminder to headteachers and teachers of the need for in-service training programmes which develop intercultural and inter-religious understanding. Extending the understanding of the cultural and religious backgrounds of pupils can underpin strongly levels of achievement.

What children, staff and others say about IEC

'The children listened with great interest. Parents of different faiths who were present found the session enjoyable and informative.'

'.... without exception the students found their visit interesting and felt that they had gained a great deal from the experience. In both the Hindu temple and the mosque we were made to feel most welcome. The individuals who took care of us spent a great deal of time giving us important information.'

'It was good to hear about customs and practices within a cultural and religious framework from someone who so obviously understood....'

The IEC has video and other material available to illustrate its work.

Theme F: Case Study 2

Multi-Level working between CD/LEI, the NGO GVC (Gruppo Volontariato Civile) and the Co-operative 'The Moon in the Well'

(See Section One Case Study 2.1, 'The Role of CD/LEI' for information about this Centre for Intercultural Education.)

Miriam Traversi, CD/LEI, Bologna
Tel: 00 39 051 300 812
Fax: 00 39 051 397 306
E-mail: Miriam.Traversi@comune.bologna.it
Website: miriam.traversi/comunedibologna/it

CD/LEI is a documentation and research centre for intercultural education (see p.47), working in a multi-level approach with a number of partners to develop and extend intercultural understanding in Bologna. Its founding partners are the Department of Education of the University of Bologna, the Provincial Education Authority for Bologna, the Municipality of Bologna (The Office of the Alderman for Education), National Trades Unions (CGIL, CISL, UIL). It works in a multi-level approach with a variety of partners, including the founders, towards the following aims:

- to address issues related to raising the quality of educational experience and achievement of ethnic minority and immigrant children in the schools of Bologna and its Province

- to develop intercultural, non-eurocentric pedagogical approaches and materials

- to develop and extend intercultural understanding, at a local and wider level, through the following and other means

    - providing lists of associations, experts, schools and teachers undertaking valuable work in these fields

    - producing and extending a catalogue of intercultural books and videos

    - providing materials related to intercultural teaching methods

    - providing in-service training for teachers, students and others.

GVC (*Gruppo Volontariato Civile* – Civil Volunteer Group) is a non-governmental organisation working in the field of International Co-operation with Developing Countries. Its main focus is on the development of projects on issues such as social welfare – for example, public health; agriculture; and safety and first aid. GVC's work in Italy also deals with information and education related to the concenpt of development.

La Luna Nel Pozzo (The Moon in the Well) is an NGO (Non-Governmental Organisation) founded in 1983. Its main activities are:

- environmental education, working with schools, public services, trades unions and state-maintained firms

- training in intercultural education, with an emphasis on the relationships between commercialism, environment and development

- developing a Documentation Centre, opened in 1994, called 'Meridian', geared towards the University of Bologna and international co-operation.

- CD/LEI places increasing importance on working with a number of partners in a multi-level approach based on a clear division and definition of roles and responsibilities among the partners. One of CD/LEI's top priorities is the organisation of in-service training and refresher courses for teachers. CD/LEI co-ordinates the courses, plans the programmes and selects the tutors and lecturers

GVC and La Luna Nel Pozzo are both partners in this major activity and valuable contributors to the subjects of the programmes. They are also excellent team-workers. La Luna Nel Pozzo deals with the technical management of the courses and collaborates over their planning, while GVC acts as a fund-raiser and provides the administration for the courses.

The **aims** of the multi-level work between the three organisations includes improving the appreciation and valuing of different cultures by bringing people together to learn from first-hand experiences of different cultures, exploring these different cultures with them and enabling them to understand the value of diversity. Also, to provide in-service training and develop projects which promote and develop intercultural education at city and regional levels.

CD/LEI's long experience in teacher training has led to a diversification of the methodology of in-service training. The three organisations have worked together to devise a variety of working practices, including small group, co-operative activities which are proving successful in actively involving teachers in the development of new teaching and learning strategies and developing co-operative approaches with a specific, practical aim. The range of training activities includes whole group and small group, co-operative exercises. The work of the groups is facilitated by members of CD/LEI and La Luna Nel Pozzo, often under the aegis of Italian experts or experts of other origins.

Teachers and other participants in the programmes have benefited greatly from the wider perspectives provided by the partners in the organisation of the in-service programmes. They have shown considerable interest in the content and processes, particularly welcoming the small group and team activities, in a context where training has traditionally been of a didactic nature.

What has been learned?

- the co-operation between the organisations has led to a better understanding of teachers' training and information needs

- the teachers want to be actively involved in the training activities

- involving teachers in small group tasks with specific aims and objectives, such as producing antiracist teaching and learning resources, is an excellent way of empowering them to implement new approaches with their pupils.

Main outcomes

- pupils are taught to be more critical as a result of teachers themselves using a more criticially reflective approach to intercultural issues

- pupils learn to move beyond stereotypical images of other cultures in a more permanent way

- pupils have a deeper understanding of subject matter as a result of considering issues from different perspectives

- achievement levels in schools have improved as pupils apply the skills they have acquired

- pupils' levels of personal and social development have been raised because they understand the value of diversity better

- teachers are empowered and motivated by the training they receive

- teachers adopt a more critical stance towards their own cultural and linguistic background

- teachers are more likely to take risks when they have developed approaches and materials themselves

- teachers acquire more competences as teachers as a result of the in-service training methods

- there is a general improvement in the quality of education provided by a school which absorbs the messages of the training

- intercultural skills have come to be considered important 'basic skills' for teachers

- the parents of ethnic minority children feel more respected and valued as a result of the implementation of new approaches arising from the training courses

- the three organisations involved – CD/LEI, La Luna Nel Pozzo and GVC – have identified a range of benefits to them:

  - they can address teachers' in-service needs more effectively
  - they can create high quality research groups of teachers around particular themes
  - their own research and knowledge base is enhanced
  - they are more skilled in communication and collaboration.

Implications for in-service training

The most important in-service training needs are as follows:

- courses in teaching Italian as a second or additional language

- knowledge about different world religions and cultures

- causes of achievement and under-achievement and progress

- means of reviewing school curriculum plans and syllabi from a non-eurocentric perspective;

- moving beyond the textbook: development of intercultural approaches and non-verbal communication strategies, using audio-visual aids, computers etc.

If the interests of ethnic minority pupils are to be well served, the following must be done at local level:

- raise awareness at government level, and lobby those who make decisions, so that there is a proper framework of legislation and funding support for initiatives and basic provision

- work closely with headteachers so that they are aware of the needs facing their teachers and pupils and so that schools and teachers can be properly equipped to cater for increasingly diverse intakes of pupils.

Theme F: Case Study 3

The Turin Intercultural Centre

City of Turin Educational Services, Luca Palese
** 39 11 442 9126 (fax)
** 39 11 442 9130 (tel)

The presence of a significant number of people from ethnic minority backgrounds is relatively recent. There has been a history of internal immigration to Turin, for example from the South of Italy. Growing numbers of people from ethnic minorities, gypsies and refugees, has led the city to promote the richness and value of diversity through a major four-year promotion in the city, including some significant intercultural events, and the city authorities have opened an intercultural centre.

The Intercultural Centre in Turin

Turin has established an Intercultural Centre in a large building (a former school) in a mixed residential suburb of the city. The decision not to locate it in a major area of ethnic minority households was deliberate. The Centre has a growing number of resources representing the cultures and faiths of people of different backgrounds and there are also displays of children's schoolwork on the theme of diversity. The resources include books and publications, artefacts and other materials. The Centre is used by groups of schoolchildren who then base work undertaken in school on the information garnered from the Centre. This is one way schools can introduce and develop intercultural education within their curriculum. There are changing exhibitions and presentations of different faiths and cultures.

The Centre serves as a training venue for courses and programmes on intercultural education, for example training in the features of different cultures and religions for teachers and other professionals. These programmes are represented in the overall programme of events organised by the city's Education Services (which do not have responsibility for statutory schooling, but provide a wide range of complementary activities to support education and learning in the city, including pre-school and adult education).

Community Associations also have a base in the Centre and the Committee of the Local Community Associations meet there. In this way, the city gives support to the Committee and the associations, and it can consult with representatives of those communities.

The Centre is:

- an Intercultural Centre which is both a symbol of the city's commitment to promoting the value of diversity and a physical manifestation of its policy in this area

- a multi-purpose centre which accommodates resources, training, displays and expertise, as well as providing a base for local community association representatives

- a valuable resource for training and for learning about different faiths and cultures, which is accessible to schools and which provides many and changing resources with which teachers and children can engage.

What has been learned?

- an Intercultural Centre in a city provides a valuable resource for people of all backgrounds and ages

- the presence of the Centre has a symbolic importance as well as practical value in terms of the potential for learning about different cultures

- it is a useful resource for schools and teachers in developing their approaches to intercultural education and it enables children and young people to find out about different cultures and faiths present in the city and elsewhere.

Implications for in-service training:

Professionals from all service areas need training in the features of different cultures and faiths. A Centre such as this can concentrate expertise and resources. Although there are significant differences between this Centre and the Interfaith Centre in Bradford, both facilities provide a particular example for other cities to consider.

Teachers can be sensitised to issues which they need to consider carefully in terms of their approach to intercultural education and the provision they and their schools make for children from diverse backgrounds. The training programmes and information available at an Intercultural Centre can assist greatly with these processes.

Theme F: Case Study 4

Training teachers in intercultural education in Athens and its region

Thalia Dragonas and Anna Frangoudaki
University of Athens, Department of Pre-School Education
Tel: ** 301 36 17 922 or ** 301 36 35 165
Fax: ** 301 36 17 922
Email: drathal@ath.forthnet.gr

Four million of the total population in Greece of 10 million live in Athens. Greece has traditionally been a country of emigration, especially between 1950 and 1970. But the last 15 years has seen a great change in Athens especially. People have arrived from Eastern Europe including the former Soviet Union and from North Africa, challenging the notion of national identity in Greece based on the idea of linguistic, religious and cultural homogeneity. Whilst there are no official statistics, the number of people from ethnic and other minorities living in Athens is estimated by the media at 600,000.

The education system is centralised and based on an ethnocentric philosophy, which means that teachers do not have any training or preparation for working with children who bring different languages and cultures to school. Most of the ethnic minority children are placed in classes designated as 'reception' classes where Greek is taught by teachers who have not acquired the methodology to teach Greek as a second language and often have a rather negative attitude towards the new arrivals.

This case illustrates the work of an interdisciplinary team which has worked in one of two schools over the past four years to address these issues. The schools are located in the centre of the city in a deprived area in which two communities live side by side but with no real contact between them. There are orthodox Greeks who speak Greek and there are Muslims of Greek origin who speak Turkish and Greek. Given the political difficulties between Greece and Turkey, any political event can heighten tensions between the two communities.

The children of the area go to the same school, where 65% speak Turkish as their first language – yet the Parents Association for the school did not have one single representative from this community. At the start of the academic year 1996/97, the Ministry of Education designated this as an 'intercultural school', according to a law passed by Parliament to develop intercultural education in Greek schools.

The programme developed in the school aimed to continue longstanding actions in support of intercultural education in the Ministry of Education and to test a pilot module of training and development. This constituted interventions which could be applied to any context and which would have a multi-level affect on school, teachers, pupils and parents.

Primary and pre-school teachers received training, in a two-stage programme on techniques and approaches. There was systematic evaluation of the interventions – a major preoccupation has been to develop a rigorous system of evaluation which can be universally applied to produce quantitative and comparable data about the effects of the actions undertaken.

Links were established between pre-school and primary education, because early interventions have proved vital. Attitudes and skills developed in pre-school education foster the integration of children from different linguistic and cultural backgrounds into the statutory school system. We worked in a crèche and a nursery school near the school, to sensitise all staff and parents to intercultural issues and ensure that the staff of the crèche and the nursery understood how they could work successfully with children from different linguistic and cultural backgrounds, using new pedagogical techniques and approaches such as group work.

This development is characterised by:

*   developing work for intercultural education in different contexts

*   an approach combining scientific research with a programme of on-going training on the ground, based on an action-research model

What has been learned?

- the pedagogical debate about intercultural education is part of the overall debate about and response to the multicultural society which is a fact of life across Europe, especially in cities

- the training of teachers and exchanges among teachers of ideas and experiences helps to create the notion of European identity and European citizenship

- serious work on the ground must be combined with rigorous, scientific and theoretical reflection

- any such activity will produce successes and failures – and it is important to learn from both

- interventions designed to address racism and xenophobia do not produce rapid results because they have to do with questions of personal identity and attitude

- one of the more difficult aspects of intercultural training programmes is changing teachers' stereotypes and persuading them to adopt new approaches to their teaching and to their role as teachers.

Main outcomes

- The nursery school has been opened up to its social environment and the needs of its communities. This has been achieved by educational activities within the nursery and through work involving the parents and the municipal authorities responsible for the school.

- An evaluation process had been developed which provided interesting results and enabled us to plan future work on the basis of the data. These evaluations are also relevant to other people training teachers in intercultural issues because the evaluation model has been demonstrated to be relevant to a wide range of contexts.

- The interdisciplinary and multi-level approach enables us to deal with many aspects of the issues – there is value in working both vertically (initial training, in-service training, research) and horizontally (work on the ground).

- Teachers are becoming more committed to the processes involved and are themselves operating as trainers in some instances. This is one way of developing a critical mass of expertise and experience in an education system

- Our approach and training programmes have been recognised as a successful pilot project by the Ministry of Education.

- Specific results have been achieved:

    - the school has been selected as a pilot school for a new programme of primary education in Greece involving all-day education

- the Ministry of Education has recognised the importance of our work and has funded us for a three year project to work on the context and processes of education of the Turskish-speaking minority in Thrace, which is important for educational, social and political reasons

- the collaboration with our European partners has enabled us to develop our experience and expertise and to participate in projects which address issues of common concern across Europe.

Implications for in-service training

- in-service training programmes need to be based on scientific research and under-pinned by a strong theoretical framework

- in-service and initial teacher training programmes in intercultural education must have access to data which demonstrates the effectiveness of the approaches adopted and enables continual evaluation of the programme

- all teachers require in-service training in intercultural issues so they can cope with the challenges of increasing diversity in the classroom.

Theme F: Case Study 5

Peer mediation at Sogn Vocational School, Oslo

SOGN Vocational School, Oslo±
Tel: ** 47 22 36 97 00
Fax: ** 47 22 36 97 01
Email: annet@sogn.vgs.no

Sogn is a vocational school with around 2,200 students, about 30% of them of ethnic minority origin. Teaching and administrative staff of the school amount to 350 people. The school draws students from all over Oslo. They come from diverse cultural, social and economic backgrounds and their previous level of education is also quite varied. So for many students the school is completely outside their community. Average class size is twelve and there are 119 different courses. About sixty different languages are represented in the school, and courses are taught in Norwegian.

This project started at Sogn in collaboration with the Mediation Board in Oslo. Sogn was granted extra resources to try to solve a difficult situation characterised by violence between young people. Preventing violence is a priority for the Norwegian school authorities. The school has now developed some competence in this field. Many young people find it difficult to adapt to the situation they find in the school, especially young people from ethnic minorities, and the school, also, has had difficulties in adapting to the needs of these young people. The result has been an unacceptable level of violence.

According to the law, every young person must be given the opportunity of continuing their education and the school authorities have to provide for this. The Mediation Board was established by law as an alternative to the traditional justice system and acts as a conflict resolution body outside the courtroom. The role of the Mediation Board is to solve conflicts by involving young people found guilty of an offence in community-based work rather than traditional punishments. Norway may be the only European country where this possibility exists. This collaboration with the Mediation Board operates at national level and the experiences from this work have been incorporated into the Sogn project.

Aims of the multi-level work at Sogn

- to reduce the number of violent incidents at the school and involving school students

- to establish mediation centres with students as peer mediators

- to provide positive role models for all students by equipping them to solve problems

- to help students from different socio-cultural backgrounds to have equal opportunities at school

- to give the students permanent skills they can use in situations throughout their lives, so that it is easier for them to function within both school and society

- to provide teachers with tools for dealing with conflict situations in classrooms.

This is a transnational project in intercultural education and it lasts for three years. The project is based on the active participation of students as peer mediators, and in internet conferences and seminars. An optional course in Peer Mediation has been developed in which both students and teachers participate. In recent years, violence at the school had increased. A project group of three people, one full-time and two part-time, has been established to tackle such incidents. The conflicts have been between different ethnic groups and Norwegians, within ethnic groups and between gangs. A new situation has developed as a result of some girls following male role models and becoming involved in violence.

Through the work of the project, hundreds of students have been given an introductory course in dealing with violent actions, bullying and harassment by using mediation techniques. This has been a compulsory part of the teaching for both students and teachers. The students have been given a thorough introduction to the concept of mediation and an explanation of why it is so important. Professional mediators have led these programmes and have inspired students and teachers. After the introductory course, all students have the option of a continuing training programme where they act as resource groups for other students. The student groups have communicated with project partners in the UK and Denmark through the internet about their experiences as mediators.

This development is characterised by:

- the great care taken to make students aware of the further positive consequences of involvement in peer mediation, for example the possibility of internet contact with the project partners and the application of skills in other subject/curriculum areas

- the training and involvement of students as peer mediators in situations which adults acting alone had had great difficulty in resolving

- the importance of developing measures through peer mediation training which prevent violence occurring in the first place.

What has been learned?

- it is important to keep records of incidents of bullying, harassment and violence and to have clear procedures for following them up

- introducing peer mediation and providing many students with life skills in this area has led to a reduction of such incidents and demonstrates its value

- both teachers and students seem to be more confident in dealing with situations which could lead to conflict

- training in peer mediation techniques has many positive features which impact on intercultural education and enable students to be more willing to learn in a range of situations

- consistent and on-going evaluation is important to ensure that the project develops in line with any trends identified as a result of evaluation.

Main outcomes

- students have acquired skills in mediation and in working with people from different cultural and linguistic backgrounds and have gained in self-confidence as a result

- teachers have also acquired basic skills in mediation. They realise that there are colleagues they can consult who may be facing similar problems. They also have a better understanding of students from different cultural backgrounds

- there are now fewer violent incidents at the school. There is closer co-operation with the Mediation Board, and the staff are more competent in dealing with difficult situations.

Theme G
Provision for Children from Cradle to School and for their Parents

Early childhood development and early intervention

Children develop most rapidly in their early years. Much depends how infants and young children are stimulated and engaged in activities involving language, socialisation and other learning. Many ethnic minority children come from homes where the processes of early childhood development are well understood and fostered, within a secure and caring family situation. But other families may be less able to promote the optimal development of their young children, for reasons such as:

*   parents being unaware of what optimises early child development, for example, the importance of talking to children in meaningful contexts and using relevant stimuli

*   difficult circumstances, especially in the case of low-income families

*   families having difficulties enabling gaining access for their children to important first-hand experiences

*   a shortage of stimulating resources at home – toys, equipment, creative materials, books

*   misunderstandings about how best to prepare children for schooling

Early intervention is recognised as important. In educational terms this generally applies to programmes after the child has started school. Baseline assessments of pupils on entry to school and pre-school indicate that there are major differences already emerging in children's development at that stage. To help ensure that children develop optimally in these vital early years a framework of support is needed to enable parents to give them the skills, knowledge and understanding they will require.

So it is essential to work with parents as early as possible in their children's lives – even before the child's birth and certainly soon thereafter. There is an obvious multi-level link here to health workers and home visitors, whose jobs are related to pregnancy and post-natal care and early learning activities. DIECEC cities have a small but growing number of innovative approaches, including arrangements for parents to learn with a skilled professional alongside their children, and schemes for health and care workers and others to provide educational materials and guidance to new parents. Where these schemes are well thought out and have specific educational aims and efficient evaluation, they can hugely enhance children's early learning.

The roles and contributions of schools and cities

Schools, cities and education systems can help most in the neighbourhoods of multiple disadvantage and stress where many ethnic minority families live. It is essential to create a multi-level approach and set up a multi-agency partnership to meet the needs of infants and their families. Senior representatives of all the services and agencies which impact on infants and their families should be involved. The partnership should be managed so it co-ordinates the work of different services and ensures coherence between them.

A considerable number and variety of professionals make contact with families for different reasons and some families encounter people from social services, health, welfare, education etc. Cities and systems have to decide whether this is an enlightened approach. Although each service may have statutory and other important issues to address with a family, it may be preferable for each family to have a key contact person who undertakes the overall liaison work with them and can explain why so many agencies approach them and co-ordinate the work of them all. In some instances, cities report that there is usually one professional who has a good relationship with the family and who can efficiently assume this role.

The city or education system will contribute also to establishing specialist staffed early childhood development centres, pre-schools and crèches which provide not just care but stimulus and development for the children and training for their parents in how to build on this at home. The centres should provide access to all the professional services working with the families. In some centres parents are now working alongside their children and a skilled professional, learning how to help them to develop. DIECEC has evidence of parents who have been involved in such schemes passing on their skills to others, gaining confidence, behaving differently towards their children and supporting their children's learning and development more effectively.

Working with very young children and their parents requires specialist training coupled with sound theoretical understanding of early childhood development. This does not yet apply in every DIECEC city. In the best practice, only trained specialists are allowed to supervise work in these contexts, with all the staff involved sharing an understanding of the processes of early learning and development.

What contribution can schools make? Some might provide the setting for training programmes, while others might at least present cogent arguments for setting up a centre in their community and help with the identification of resources. In some communities, a suitable resource may already exist in embryonic form; multi-level working and co-operation between agencies can help it to develop. It is greatly in schools' interests, as indicated below, for children to be helped in a meaningful way before they begin school. Strong links between formal schooling and early years provision help schools to understand the children's needs and levels of development better when they arrive, and to foster better mutual understanding of policy and practice.

Benefits of early intervention

There is clear evidence that children who have received good nursery education achieve better all round than children who have not. There is also a lasting positive effect in, for example, social skills and attitudes to other people and work. DIECEC does not yet have evidence that the same applies to children who have been involved in the programmes described but it is reasonable to suppose that it will. There is, however, already evidence of the benefit to parents of their involvement in these schemes and of the associated short-term benefits for children.

This theme is therefore presented as an area for further exploration and development, but also as a potential priority – as a preventative and developmental measure which can bring wider advantages to communities. The value of investing in early childhood development cannot be overestimated, and in considering the resourcing implications of extending their provision, cities should regard financial and other resources required as an investment rather than a cost. Interestingly, the DIECEC cities which make the strongest provision in this area through their own resources are mostly those which do not have a formal responsibility for the statutory school system.

The need to prioritise early learning facilities and programmes in regeneration schemes

The priority for establishing such centres must obviously be areas of greatest disadvantage and with the poorest educational attainment. DIECEC calls on all regeneration schemes, however funded, to prioritise the need to invest in centres and programmes which enable parents to develop their skills and provide facilities which can better support their children's early and subsequent learning.

The case for this has never been stronger. Evidence from regeneration activities demonstrates that investment in human infrastructure is vital. Investing only in training for the short or longer-term unemployed will not break the cycle of low educational achievement. Regeneration programmes provide a significant opportunity for multi-level and multi-agency working, marshalling resources to provide a framework for supporting parents and improving the early learning of children in ways which will leave these processes and facilities embedded in communities and raise the threshold of achievement.

Theme G: Case Study I

Infant education provided by the Comunidad de Madrid in public (state) schools

Amador Sanchez and Jose Antonio Luengo
Tel: Amador Sanchez: ** 34 91 580 41 74
Tel: Jose A. Luengo: ** 34 91 580 41 82
Fax: ** 34 91 580 4173
E-mail: jose.vargas@comadrid.es

Infant/Early Years Education in Spain

In October, 1990 the overall education system up to university level was reorganised in line with new legislation. Arrangements for early years education, from birth to the start of statutory schooling (which begins at age 6) were incorporated into a phase entitled 'Infant Education'. (Note: *Educacion Infantil* best translates as 'Early Years Education', appearing to be interpreted in the same way in Spanish and English-speaking contexts.)

Educacion Infantil now constitutes the first phase of the education system. It is divided into two stages, from 0-3 and from 3-6 years when compulsory schooling begins. It is voluntary. However, it is fundamentally different from arrangements for pre-school care or child-minding that generally characterise provision for young children: there must be a strong, unequivocal element of education and learning in the provision made.

The '*Casas de Ninos*' (Pre-school classes) provided by the Comunidad de Madrid

The Comunidad de Madrid (the Region of Madrid) does not yet have formal responsibility for the statutory system of schooling but will do so when Madrid becomes one of the autonomous regions of Spain during 1999. Meanwhile, the Comunidad makes provision for pre-school education, and also additional learning opportunities for children and young people and further education and training for adults, with a priority for areas of socio-economic disadvantage.

The Comunidad understands that areas of disadvantage in Madrid for the provision of pre-school and nursery classes need priority, so it situates them in areas where many ethnic minority families live. The overall social policy of Madrid is to create balanced communities, avoiding as far as possible a heavy concentration of ethnic minority families in one particular area or school.

The Comunidad funds 79 *Casa de Ninos* (pre-school classes), all staffed by specialist early childhood educators and teachers. It is part of the co-operation agreement operated by the Comunidad, the *Direccion Provincial* and the *Ayutamientos* (Local Municipal Authorities). The co-operation with the Direccion Provincial is particularly significant in securing the location of the classes in primary schools and integration with them in terms of continuity of learning.

The policy and practice of the Comunidad de Madrid

The Comunidad de Madrid understands the vital importance of early intervention in children's development especially for families of significant social, economic and educational disadvantage, so it invests considerably in pre-school and nursery education. The Direccion Provincial, responsible for statutory schooling, appreciates the advantage of locating pre-school and nursery classes in primary schools where buildings allow. Transition from nursery to primary education becomes smoother, children are better prepared for school, links have already been established.

Many of the pre-schools and nurseries offer great flexibility: there is often early-morning care so that parents can leave their children on their way to work; there are facilities for children to sleep at the school during the day; the educators are trained to work with children on an individual basis so the school can respond to children with particular needs.

Educacion Infantil aims to develop in very young children the following abilities:

* to know about their own bodies and how to use them

* to develop relationships with others through different forms of communication and expression

* to observe and explore their natural, family and social environment

* to develop independence in everyday activities.

The *Casos de Ninos* should

* provide educational opportunities which help to compensate for differences in social, economic and cultural background and prevent learning difficulties in future phases of education

* work with families to create links between home and school and to support the educational progress of their children.

The pedagogical approach employed in the *Casa de Ninos* is characterised by first-hand experience, activity, structured play, and learning by doing in the company of trained early childhood educators. The staff of the centres plan and organise the learning experiences as a team. The curriculum and educational activities are based on an integrated approach. All the facets of children's lives are reflected in the learning situations and experiences. The curriculum is structured around:

- developing their personal identity and autonomy/independence

- their social and physical development

- communication and representation, where children learn to interact with different forms and means of communication and representation through different media and use them to represent and express their thoughts and feelings.

This development is characterised by:

- the commitment of the Comunidad de Madrid to providing high quality early learning experiences for as many children from disadvantaged backgrounds as possible, including many ethnic minority children

- the specialist nature of the provision, made by appropriately qualified and experienced staff

- the co-operation with the Direccion Provincial over the location of pre-school and nursery classes in primary schools

- multi-level and multi-agency working, the latter with other professionals who support the children and their families (for example, social services)

- the involvement and engagement of families in the development of the *Casas de Ninos* and the involvement of parents living in the areas in which they are situated.

What has been learned?

- initiatives in the *Casas de Ninos* in which children, parents and educators from different cultural backgrounds have together found out about different cultures, ways of life and values have been hugely enriching. Children thus gain an early appreciation of the value of different cultures

- providing workshop activities on a weekly basis during the afternoon and early evening for the children and their families has allowed their parents to learn to work together with them and each other and to pursue similar activities at home and outside

- children's language development and their ability to work with different resources are accelerated by attendance at the *Casas de Ninos*

- the transition into statutory schooling is much easier for both children and their parents

- it is vital to have specialist-trained early childhood educators working with very young children. (Note: DIECEC cannot emphasise this enough!)

Main outcomes

Pupils: the self-esteem and confidence of the children attending the *Casas de Ninos* are noticeably enhanced. Typically, they will say '*Yo lo se hacer*' (I know how to do that). Their basic skills are enhanced: language, independence, personal hygiene, feeding themselves, learning skills. Their language develops particularly through structured play and role-play. Their ability to understand basic rules and to accept the norms of behaviour is enhanced, as is their ability to work and play with others.

Teachers/educators: are motivated and gain professional satisfaction from working with the families as well as the children; along with their specialist training, they have acquired new skills in working with children from diverse backgrounds. Their professional development has also been enhanced as a result of working with other professionals.

The schools incorporating the *Casas de Ninos*: the collaboration between professionals from different backgrounds clarifies roles and responsibilities and people value their own and others' roles more. The schools develop a better understanding of the needs and possibilities of development for children up to age 6 and what they can expect of them. By working with colleagues in the *Casa de Ninos* they discover different ways of achieving the same objectives. In most cases, the school is able to make consistent and coherent provision for children aged from 1 to 12.

The families: they become more confident: they ask questions, participate in activities and confide in the professional staff of the school. They come into the school regularly. They know what they can expect of their children at different ages, how they can share games with them and help them to develop at home. The families develop a feeling of solidarity, realising that many of them have the same needs, and they value the opportunity to meet other families with their children in a pleasant environment.

The City district: elected representatives recognise and are able to represent positively the value of early childhood education. Facilities for community activities are improved. *The Casas de Ninos* help to develop a sense of community and of mutual responsibility and interdependence.

Implications for in-service training

Specialised programmes of training are needed for people working with very young children, relating to pedagogy, methodology, relationships etc. Entry requirement in Spain is for a higher level vocational qualification (completion of higher level secondary education (baccalaureat) plus two years further training). The teacher training qualification must have a specialism in *Educacion Infantil*. There should also be continuing in-service training related to developing pedagogy and innovation, since the headteacher of the school, the leader of the *Casa de Ninos* and all the staff involved need to know and understand different cultures and the backgrounds of the children. There is also a need for training in working with parents and families and with professionals from other backgrounds.

What children, staff or others involved in the Project or development work have said:

(translated from Spanish)

'I was worried at the start of the workshops for parents but now I feel at home in them'.

'If I had stayed at home with my son during the first few years he spent at the school, he would have missed a great deal.'

'My daughter wants to go to the school on Saturdays and Sundays as well!'

'Next year, when my son will no longer be in the *Casa de Ninos* but in the main school – will I still be able to come to the workshops for parents?'

And a teacher from the main school said: 'This facility (the *Casa de Ninos*) ought to be available in every school'.

Theme G: Case Study 2

Provision for very young children in Bologna

Franca Marchesi and Gabriele Ventura
Settore Istruzione-Sport
Municipality of Bologna
Municipal Department of Education
Via Oberdan 24, Bologna
Tel: 00 39 051 204 651/204 695
Fax: 00 39 051 204 679

Miriam Traversi: CD LEI (Centro Documentazione/Laboratorio Educazione Interculturale)
Tel: 0039 051 300 812
Fax: 00 39 051 397 306
E-mail: Miriam.Traversi@comune.bologna.it

Bologna has a significant and growing ethnic minority population. There is considerable demand for early childhood education, and Bologna has responded. The city operates 192 crèches and pre-school learning centres committed to caring for young children and helping them to develop. The city is alert to the vital role of parents in early learning, and is developing ways of involving parents more in activities which help them to foster their children's learning and development. Whilst this early childhood provision is not made especially for ethnic minority families, there is no doubt that the overall context of high quality early opportunities for learning greatly benefits ethnic minority children.

Bologna ensures that early childhood care and education is provided by specialist educators and early childhood staff who understand the processes of early child development and can provide high quality care and opportunities for learning. The city has set up a number of creches and nursery schools with good ratios of expert staff to children: 1:4 for children aged 0-1; 1:6 for children aged 1-3; 1:25 for children aged 4-6.

In 1994, all pre-school provision was co-ordinated through *The Integrated Public System*, which includes municipal, state and private providers of pre-school education. The municipal nursery schools offer reduced fees for low income families.

There are 46 full time and 8 part time crèches for children aged 3 months-3 years. 2,037 children are enrolled full time and 198 part time, which means that 30.37% of a total population of 7,358 under threes are on roll. Of the nursery schools, which cater for age 3-5 years, there are 205 municipal kindergartens/nurseries, 19 state nurseries and 49 private nurseries. Virtually all the children in Bologna are on roll: 73.5% in the municipal nurseries, 7.0% in state nurseries and 18.8% in the private nurseries.

The crèches and nursery schools are based on the philosophy of learning through experience so as to develop children's language, social, motor and other learning skills and afford large spaces and stimulating environments. The staff provide individualised support for children according to individual needs. The curriculum is based on the need for young children to have a wide range of opportunities within areas of experience that involve language, number, creativity, physical development, socialisation, investigation and problem-solving and the use of structured play.

A significant development that is beginning to spread is the closer involvement of parents in learning alongside their children. Parents agree to attend some of the sessions each week and work alongside staff, learning from them how they can help their child develop at home.

Aims of the Creches and Nursery Schools

- to provide a high quality, specialised early childhood care and learning environment

- to ensure that the support for children and parents comes from specialist, trained and qualified staff

- to provide a stimulating learning environment

- to provide an individualised curriculum for each child

- to involve parents directly as much as possible in the development of their child and in the activities of the centre.

In each crèche, a team made up of nursery nurses, the educational co-ordinator and crèche workers is supported by specialist therapists as needed for individual children's language and other development difficulties. These specialists include a psychologist, a pediatrician and medical specialists. Underpinning the provision is a philosophy that children begin to develop cognitive processes very early in their lives. But that this should not mean that early learning should be formal. Language development, for example, is not about memorisation but the understanding of meaning. Emphasis is on communication and on individual children's personal development styles – their individual perception, exploration and learning styles.

The role of the team of adults is to create contexts which enable children to make discoveries and create links between different areas of cognitive development. The adults operate as directors (akin to the role of film director), setting up stimulating situations in the expressive, logical-arithmetical and linguistic domains.

This development is characterised by:

* provision of high quality care and learning opportunities for very young children provided by specialist staff in a suitable environment

* sessions in which parents work and learn alongside their children

* the development of children as independent, autonomous learners, supported by careful curriculum planning

* a high level of support for children's linguistic development

* early, accelerated development of the second or additional language

* there is on-going monitoring and assessment of children's development and how effectively the parents are using the same methodologies at home.

What has been learned?

* a methodology which involves the parents as well as the children is fundamental

* by playing with their children in an environment where they have the support and guidance of trained early years specialists, parents learn with their children and learn also how to play with them in a developmental and non-stereotyped way (for example, the same toys are used with girls and boys, and the parents learn to treat both genders in the same way).

Main outcomes

Pupils: children's self-esteem is enhanced through the non-directive pedagogical guidance provided by the specialist staff. They are empowered to learn independently and to develop personally and as learners. The teaching and learning of basis skills is skillfully integrated with the process of developing awareness and understanding their environment.

Teachers: teachers are well motivated by the relatively autonomous and highly creative environment of the pre-school provision. The educational policies enhance their self-esteem and personal and social development is enhanced by the activities they plan and execute with ethnic minority and Italian parents.

Parents: parent's self-esteem, language skills and personal and social development are supported by their involvement with their children's pre-school education. Many parents now participate regularly in the crèche and nursery schools' activities (fairs, parties, exhibitions of children's work, cultural activities). Parents are invited to share their expertise (for example, in arts and crafts) with teachers and children, and this affirms them and helps children to see them as important figures in their education. Parents also participate in meetings held by teachers on educational issues, such as how to support children's language development.

Municipal Education Department: the successes of the pre-school provision mean that the Department is seen as a significant player in the world of pre-school education.

Implications for in-service training

- since 1970, there has been a programme of in-service training for all teachers and other staff in pre-school provision – both refresher courses and programmes which focus on new issues

- the range of programmes includes working in partnerships with children's parents and addressing specific intercultural issues, the latter in collaboration with CD/LEI and involving people from the ethnic minority communities.

- This focus on in-service training is essential to the continuing development of the work of pre-school provision in Bologna.

Theme H
Provision for Children and Young People at Risk of School Failure, and Second Chance Schooling

As indicated in the Key Aims and Principles set out in Section One, the numbers of young people failing to complete statutory education or finishing up with poor or no qualifications is worryingly high. It needs to be addressed through both preventative and responsive, curative measures which provide 'second chance' opportunities for young people to gain qualifications. In most DIECEC cities, ethnic minority pupils are over-represented in these statistics.

DIECEC cities are responding pragmatically. There will always be some children and young people who fail, for reasons which may not even be due to the education system, so 'second chance' opportunities will always be required. But everything possible must be done to prevent failure – the objective must be to get it right the first time.

Second Chance Schooling and Education

DIECEC identifies two types of provision needed to enable young people to qualify for further (and possibly higher) education, training and employment – within existing schools or at special centres.

1. Second chance education in existing or 'normal' schools or colleges

Provision is made in existing schools which responds to the needs of underachieving and disaffected pupils and, although they may still underachieve in relation to their potential, the damage will be limited. The features of these second chance opportunities within the statutory school system are likely to be:

- a close relationship established between each young person and a particular adult, probably but not always a teacher, who will encourage attendance at school and a consistent engagement with learning and will strive to build up the self-esteem and confidence of the pupil

- the involvement of positive peer and other adult role models, possibly a mentor from outside school and a peer mentor in the school

- the involvement of the home and community in scaffolding a pupil's learning and development outside school through the mentor or by other means

- an immediate focus on ensuring a level of success in specific activities undertaken in school which is then recognised and valued, as part of the process of re-engaging the pupils and building their confidence

- a focus on providing an individualised programme as part or all of the curriculum, involving the key adult along with the pupil in decisions about the programme

- depending on the nature of the pupil's needs, a focus on basic skills, especially oracy and literacy, numeracy and information technology – which could initially take up as much as half the pupil's time

- opportunities for learning which seek to identify or respond to the areas of intelligence in which the pupil is most competent and interested. Some pupils may have well-developed musical or creative ability, for example, others practical intelligence, problem-solving or physical intelligence. These approaches should also be used by the school to explore which could help to raise achievement right across their learning

- pupils taking responsibility for their own learning and being involved in the construction of their individualised curriculum

- work in one or more vocational areas or in pre-vocational skills, depending on the age, interest and aptitude of the pupil, but without assuming that this is the answer to the pupil's progression needs

Within this framework, and especially in the case of ethnic minority pupils, DIECEC identifies the following as crucial:

- the role and approach of the key adult – a good relationship is essential to re-engaging disaffected and seriously under-achieving pupils

- support for learning outside as well as in school – good work done in the 15% of time spent in school can easily be undone by negative influences outside

- identifying and responding to pupils' more strongly developed intelligences

- pupils taking increasingly high levels of responsibility for themselves and their own learning

- raising self-esteem and recognising and valuing genuine achievement.

One of the many practical issues that arise for schools in terms of responding to pupils – often 'inherited' from other schools or situations – is making suitable provision within their resources (especially when there are more than a few) without reducing provision for other pupils. DIECEC suggests that the multi-level approach is part of the answer, and that resources from different services and organisations need to be assembled and co-ordinated to help to meet these pupils' needs.

2. Specific Second Chance schools

The DIECEC cities have not been directly involved in any of the second chance schools established on the initiative of the European Union. The case for establishing such provision is clear: not only do large numbers of young people fail in current European education systems, but many find returning to the same sort of establishment in which (or maybe in their view because of which) they failed the first time, is neither attractive nor realistic. DIECEC therefore sees the notion of second chance schools as important because it provides an opportunity to develop new sorts of educational institutions which can make a valuable contribution to re-engaging many younger and older people with education and training and can also provide a laboratory for different approaches to teaching and learning. These new approaches ought to be evaluated and the successful ones disseminated to statutory school systems to help develop their provision. Second chance schools need to be very different institutions from schools run under statutory systems.

If different approaches work well in second chance schools, ought they not to be reflected in statutory schooling systems? Second chance schools which respond successfully to different forms of intelligence must have something to offer other schools. DIECEC believes that in the end, the importance of second chance schools may lie more in this direction than in their continuing existence as separate institutions. If second chance schools are to be radically different from 'statutory' schools, what would the main differences be? DIECEC suggests that second chance schools need to:

- be open learning institutions which unite under one roof the providers of a wide range of learning and training opportunities

- be institutions which see family learning as an important part of their work: parents, children, young people, grandparents learning together

- have management systems which encourage and provide for maximum flexibility of provision and response to local needs and support for individuals

- have community management or/and governance that ensures that they maintain their focus and meet local needs

- reflect notions of multiple intelligence and develop new approaches to teaching and learning with emphasis on information and communications technology (ICT)

- be institutions which offer a range of ways of improving basic skills and achieving employment-related competences corresponding to opportunities in the local labour market

- offer an environment and learning climate radically different from those normally associated with schools, or indeed with colleges of further education.

DIECEC does not believe that second chance schools should cater only for people who have failed. People in this category need to be working alongside role models for learning and have tutors who have empathy with their situation. Second chance programmes need to be available within broader-based institutions which offer learning opportunities to a wide range of people: Lifelong Learning Centres might best describe them. The case studies which follow demonstrate some of the approaches to both preventative measures and second chance education which DIECEC has seen to be effective.

Theme H: Case Study I

The Puerta Bonita Training Centre of the Comunidad de Madrid in Puerta Bonita, Carabanchel, Madrid

Comunidad de Madrid: Maria-Jesus Garrido, Rosa Maneru Mendez
Centro de la Puerta Bonita: Jose Luis Gordo Blanco
Maria Jesus Garrido and Rosa Maneru Mendez
Tel: ** 34 91 580 41 54
Fax: ** 34 91 580 41 59
E-mail: crepa@mad.servicom.es

Jose Luis Gordo Blanco
Tel: ** 34 525 14 02
Fax: ** 34 525 14 02

Some young people in the city and metropolitan area of Madrid who do not relate well to school are from ethnic minority backgrounds. For reason which may relate to their previous educational experience, their difficulty in adapting to the Spanish educational system and their recent arrival in Madrid, they do not complete school with good qualifications and some young people come to Madrid having never attended school.

Guarantees of social support deriving from current educational legislation mean that young people who have not completed statutory education can access vocational training in order to help them in the labour market. The social support programmes of the

Comunidad de Madrid identify the following objectives for educating young people in this situation:

- developing their self-esteem and confidence in their own abilities, and increasing their aspirations, expectations and ability to achieve short-term goals

- helping to address their attitudinal and emotional difficulties

- improving their adaptability, social and interpersonal skills

- instilling attitudes and abilities which will enable them to use their spare time constructively.

The training process used emphasises individual progress from a baseline which identifies each individual's strengths and weaknesses. In this sense the programme responds flexibly to the particular needs of each trainee. It is a personalised process which seeks to redress the effects of previous experiences, generally of failure. This programme is in place in the socially and economically most disadvantaged areas of the city. This case study is of the Puerta Bonita Centre, which takes its name from the district.

The Training Centre makes special provision for young people who have not achieved any qualifications by age 15/16. The building has been renovated to simulate a commercial production centre or workshop, provide spaces for meetings, study, tutorials, small group activities etc. The buildings have little in common with a conventional school. The three vocational workshops: catering, carpentry and horticulture, are capable of simulating real working situations: for example, waitering skills can be practiced in real contexts.

The staff consists of a co-ordinator and five workshop staff, three tutors/basic skills teachers and an employer-links officer who works with the firms which employ the trainees at the end of the first phase of their training. The 69 young men and 19 young women who attend are 16-18 years old. Many have not pursued education or training for some time; some have behaviour and psychological difficulties; some have learning difficulties. Approximately 20% of the trainees are from ethnic minority backgrounds. Thirteen trainees have had virtually no education; 25 have been on the roll of more than two schools and 76 have a level of education below that expected of 13 year-olds. Several of the trainees are in the care of the local authority or other institutions.

The provision involves individual tutoring by a skilled and empathetic tutor, classes in literacy, numeracy and other basic and key skills, Spanish as a second language and employment-related and specific vocational skills. The team at the Centre works in multi-level partnerships with Social Services Departments, Carabanchel, the Support Service for Young Children, the Probation Service, schools and education centres in the district and immigrant organisations. The intention is to bring together the different influences which affect the young people and to bring coherence to the young people's relationship with the training centre, the family and social services. The main educational goal is to work out a personal development plan with the young person, recognising achievements and suggesting new ways forward.

The training provided in the workshops reflects the training undertaken by professionals in that area; activities are based on real situations in employment. Basic skills education seeks to equip the trainees with the reading, writing and numeracy skills required for work in their vocational area and they are required to apply them in their vocational work.

The culmination of the programme is a guaranteed six month period of employment. This employment contract is supported by the Department of Education of the Comunidad de Madrid and the young person is supported during this period by the Puerta Bonita Centre. In several cases, this initial period of employment has turned into a permanent job.

As an incentive to undertake and continue the training programme, the trainees receive a monthly allowance of 17,000 pesetas (c.100 ecus). This may be reduced if the trainees fail to attend without good reason, or for other reasons which are agreed with each trainee at the start of their training programme.

This development is characterised by:

- interdisciplinary working in all the education and training activities is the common factor

- tutorial work which aims to support personal and social development as well as basic education

- relating the development of basic skills to the requirements of the workplace

- interdisciplinary working that underpins the work of the staff, who plan the vocational, educational and tutorial elements of the programme together. Workshop staff and teachers of the basic skills programmes are also tutors for a small group of trainees, and the employer-links person plans with the rest of the staff

- workshop activities which seek to simulate real working activities and practices

- workshop products designed and made to meet the needs and specifications of municipal services, schools or non-profit-making associations. Specifications are given by 'customers' who also set deadlines.

What has been learned?

The most important outcome from the point of view of the Training Centre is that the trainees consider the Centre to be a valuable institution, one which they want to attend and which belongs to them. They also consider that they have important and good relationships with the staff.

For the teachers, the most rewarding result is to see the trainees developing the skills they need to pursue work, acquiring skills and knowledge they did not possess when they started and, especially, growing in maturity and personal responsibility. The programme demonstrates that the situation of such young people can be successfully addressed by a combination of empathetic tutoring and work-related vocational training which supports personal, social and vocational skills development.

Developing and maintaining positive relationships with parents and guardians and harmonising the triangle of trainee, parent/guardian, school or Centre is an important learning point.

Main outcomes

The **trainees'** self-esteem is considerably enhanced by the way they are treated. The staff treat them as individuals, seek and value their opinions and handle the strengths and weaknesses of their work in a developmental way.

The **parents and guardians** of the trainees have a totally different relationship with the Training Centre to the negative one previously experienced with the schools. Parents visit the Centre for positive reasons, for example, to be served a meal prepared by the trainees, to see products they have made and observe their progress. The continuing positive relationship between the Centre and the parents helps to develop or maintain positive relationships between parents and their children.

The **teachers and tutors** usually volunteer to be placed in such a Centre because they are sympathetic to the situation of the trainees. They see their work as difficult but full of possibilities and as highly rewarding when the young people succeed on their own terms. They have learnt the importance of recognising the progress of the trainees, however small this may appear to be.

Implications for in-service training

The teachers and tutors employed in these centres must initially have the usual basic training for vocational, basic skills or tutoring work. But they also need to understand and be trained in the methodologies which will enable them to interact successfully with young people who have been excluded from the educational system and have negative attitudes towards it. Also all the staff need to understand the importance of close collaboration and team-working, and of interdisciplinary work with other services working with the young people and their families or guardians.

What the trainees, staff and others said
(translated from the Spanish quotations)
'My life has changed since I came here.'
'I have learned a trade.'
'All the staff were friendly.'
'The teachers are very committed.'
'I have got to know a lot of people – I would like to stay for another year.'
'I have learned a lot from the teachers.'

Theme H: Case Study 2

The Danish Efterskole

Odense, Denmark: Kirsten Wandall, Annette Winther
Tel: 00 45 66 148 814 (pause) 5101
Fax: 00 45 66 140 430
E-mail: KFW@odense.dk

As in all other DIECEC cities, a certain number of young people aged 15/16 do not achieve a basic level of qualification at the end of statutory schooling. This can be for a number of reasons, including disaffection with the school system, infrequent attendance and, in the case of ethnic minority children, arrival in Odense at a late age in statutory schooling. Many of the children attending an *Efterskole* have learning difficulties or other special educational needs. The *Efterskole* specialise in curricula which respond to the needs of particular students and can provide a valuable step towards a professional or educational qualification as a result of a two-year course. The *Efterskole* are not just for young people experiencing difficulties; many of them cater for young people who want to live away from home for some time, or who wish to explore areas which they cannot do at ordinary school or who have a specific interest in an area such as art or music.

The *Efterskole* are free and independent boarding schools subsidised by the govern-ment, and parents and the municipality pay for the education provided. The concept of education and training are closely connected with those of the folk high school; the objective is primarily to develop the personality of the students in co-operation with the teachers and other students. Co-operation and fellowship are therefore important features of an *Efterskole* in both formal education settings and the students' leisure time. Common duties such as care and maintenance for the building are undertaken as part of creating a climate of fellowship.

In Denmark there are 240 *Efterskole* catering for an average of 85 students each. Each school has its own specific climate and 'concept'. Some place great emphasis on areas such as sport, music, drama and outdoor activities. Others offer the possibility of achieving a school leaving certificate and still others specific provision to meet special educational needs. Some of the *Efterskole* are attached to religious denominations, political groups and professional organisations – others are totally independent.

Some of the *Efterskole* provide, in effect, second chance schooling, especially for students with learning difficulties and other special educational needs. They provide a curriculum which is often very practical and visual in its initial representation to students. These *Efterskole* are based on the theory of multiple intelligences developed by Howard Gardner. They know from comments made by students that many find it difficult to respond in terms of literacy and rationally-based intelligence, which are often weaker areas for them; conversely, the students often relate much better to visual, musical, practical and physical activities and find these better ways into learning.

Main characteristics of the pedagogy of the *Efterskole*

The teaching and learning styles used in these special kinds of *Efterskole* are therefore often different from those used in 'normal' schools. The teachers/tutors empathise with the students, understand that they have different learning needs and different forms of intelligence, and seek to respond to their strengths rather than accentuating their weaknesses. A great deal of attention is paid to improving the students' self-esteem by recognising and valuing their achievements and by valuing them as people. Students receive excellent care as well as a range of activities which challenge them and engage them in learning. Their participation in joint duties such as maintenance and cleaning and other practical tasks contributes to their feelings of success when their work is recognised and appreciated by teachers and their peers.

A considerable amount of personal tutoring is involved in the learning processes and activities. The students are encouraged to take responsibility for their own learning, once they have grasped the basic concepts and are aware of other factors (for example, health and safety considerations). The students' achievements are recorded in a number of ways and the schools make particular efforts to ensure that students' achievements are recognised and valued.

What has been learned?

*   it is important for schools and education systems to respond to different forms of intelligence through the types of schools and their curricula – suggesting that schools should be differentiated by the curriculum they offer rather than by their status

*   improving self-esteem and motivation for learning are vital to achievement

*   learners need to be enabled to take responsibility for their own learning, but this means supporting them carefully while they are learning the skills required to do so

*   where students have failed or are failing, it is especially important to scaffold their whole development – as learners and as people

*   alternative routes to further education, training and employment are essential for students who, for whatever reason, have not succeeded in compulsory education

*   some of the above need to be considered in terms of their application to the statutory school system in order to prevent earlier failure rather than having to address it at the age of 16.

Main outcomes

*   many students at the *Efterskole* make considerable progress with their educational experience in personal and social development, basic skills and vocational skills

- For many students the *Efterskole* provide an effective bridge between failure at school and the need for a threshold level of qualifications or evidence of acquired skills to access further education, training and employment

- there is the possibility of feedback from the *Efterskole* to the statutory school system to seek to ensure that there is a better response to pupils whose needs are not currently met by the normal school system.

Implications for in-service training:

Teachers at the Efterskoles need particular understandings, skills and attitudes in order to respond to the needs of their students. Training can be provided but a basic level of empathy with such students is needed as a starting point. Teachers in the statutory school system need opportunities to consider the application of methods used in the *Efterskole* to their teaching situation in ordinary schools.

Videos about individual Efterskoles are available from:
Efterskolernes Sekretariat
Farvergade 27
1463 Kobenhavn K
DK – Denmark.
Tel: 00 45 33 12 86 80
Fax: 00 45 33 93 80 94
Email: Sekretariat@efterskole.dk

Theme 1
Pathways to further and higher education, training and employment

Many young people from ethnic minorities experience considerable difficulties in accessing training, further education and, vitally, employment. The reasons. are legion – students may

- have experienced racism and had doors closed to them because of ignorance and prejudice

- have poor educational achievement at the end of formal or statutory schooling

- not received information and guidance about appropriate and further education

- not understand the basic skills and attitudes expected of them

- have cultural and religious requirements which restrict their access to opportunities

- hold unrealistic expectations of their possibilities for progression – as may parents.

- Furthermore, stereotypes held about ethnic minority youngsters may cause them to be steered down inappropriate paths or be rejected on spurious grounds.

All this presents a major challenge for cities, schools, parents, the young people themselves and providers of further education and training opportunities. Underachievement at school becomes a harsh reality at or even before age 16 or 17. Lack of access to opportunities, and especially to the labour market, condemns most young people with low or no qualifications to life at the margins of society.

This could be a powder keg for the future. Some DIECEC cities have already experienced the violent unrest caused by the frustrations of young ethnic minority people at their lack of employment and other opportunities. Such situations may well result from the lack of effective earlier interventions as suggested in the other themes in this section, and are symptoms rather than causes of a broader issue. They have to be addressed.

Co-ordinated approaches to pathways post 15/16

A multi-agency approach is required by schools, further education and training institutions, careers and guidance services, employers, trades unions, voluntary sector organisations and the young people themselves. Only the city or education and training system is likely to be in a position to create coherence and bring about the appropriate levels of cooperation between these different potential partners. In the many situations where basic and vocational education are organised and administered by different bodies, there is a particular need for the organisations involved to work closely together. In some DIECEC cities, a co-ordination group involving representatives of these and other organisations meets on a regular basis to agree actions which provide better pathways and more coherent opportunities, including the possibility of transfer from one pathway to another. These groups are either focused on the specific needs of ethnic minority and other disadvantaged young people, or on general issues to do with education and training at this transitional stage, within which the specific needs of ethnic minority youngsters can be taken into account.

The importance of good data

We have seen that data about progression routes and the situations and destinations of young people between the ages of 16 and 24 are vital to any city or system which takes on this challenge. It is especially important to have access to reliable differentiated data about the qualifications and progression routes of young people from ethnic minority backgrounds. There also needs to be reliable and up-to-date information about the labour market, including shorter and longer-term opportunities for employment. Flexible arrangements are needed for training schemes to meet the needs of employers and respond to the situations of young people who could access them.

What cities and education and training systems need to address

Not enough time is spent listening to young people from ethnic minorities and recognising their needs in relation both to education and training and to their general perceptions of their lives. Two types of studies have shown themselves to be particularly interesting and potentially useful as far as older teenagers are concerned. The first is large-scale surveys of young people, such as the UK Youth Cohort Survey, which is tracking year groups of 16 year-olds over five years with a focus on education, training and employment. This type of survey can provide much useful information about the young people's:

- understanding of systems and levels of qualifications
- career preferences

- the degree of match between aspirations and qualifications

- perceptions of different areas of employment

- the value of guidance and counselling

- the levels of support received at home.

Within such studies, 'focus groups' (for example, young ethnic minority people, ethnic minority girls, boys from a particular community) can be established for particular purposes. Meetings between the researchers and the young people can provide valuable information which can be used to improve provision for their successors.

Secondly, smaller-scale, in-depth studies of a more local nature can identify and help in prioritising specific needs. Such work can inform provision made by a whole education system. For example, the need for more opportunities to learn Finnish as a second language figured as a high priority for the young people in Helsinki – higher than had been anticipated.

Specific provision for young ethnic minority people

Within the broader theme of ensuring specific opportunities to achieve some level of qualification for young people who have failed at school, education and training systems need to put in place specific opportunities for young people from ethnic minorities. These programmes should cover issues such as:

- reintegration with education and training (for example, through mentoring or mediation schemes)

- courses in the second or additional language

- other basic skills programmes

- improving self-esteem and self-confidence

- providing vocational training opportunities

- positive action programmes which enable ethnic minority youngsters to access training programmes for which they may not have the precise requirements due to disruption of their basic education.

Within these programmes, specific attention needs to be given to the needs of refugee youngsters who have recently arrived in a city or system and who do not have the threshold qualifications necessary for progression – again because their education has been disrupted, or because they have had little education in their country of origin. It may have very little to do with their ability or willingness to learn. Access to trauma therapy is also necessary.

The importance of guidance and counselling

These programmes need to provide flexible pathways towards qualifications for young people, including arrangements which enable them to sample a number of vocational areas before making a choice. These pathways and the preparation for them must include a strong element of guidance and counselling. In circumstances where the education and training system is new to a young person, this guidance and counselling needs to be provided by people who are able to understand the situation of the young person and the systems which operate.

Trained mediators and counsellors from the ethnic minority communities have an important role to play here. Many cities or the organisations responsible for careers education, guidance and counselling, ensure through their recruitment policies that such staff exist and where this is so, high quality training must be given to them to ensure that they are able to respond to the needs of young people from ethnic minorities. Where cultural mediators or others with a more general role in counselling and working with young people are involved, it is vital that they work with up-to-date information about training and labour market opportunities and the qualifications required. In some instances, it may be best for a trained careers and guidance person to work alongside a cultural mediator so that they can learn from each other as well as guiding the young people concerned.

Guidance and counselling need to take into account the potential rather than current level of achievement of the young person. Arrangements which provide pathways towards only low-level vocational programmes should be reconsidered and better options made available. Cities and systems have constantly to bear in mind that although such arrangements may have an initial additional cost, this is likely to be low compared with the cost and consequences of providing no opportunites or unsuitable ones.

Access to a broad range of employment opportunities

A specific issue for many ethnic minority groups in European cities, including longer established communities, is the range of training and employment opportunities which they consider appropriate. There is evidence from a number of cities that some groups see only a limited range of careers as suitable for their children. Often, the entry criteria for these careers are unrealistic for most young people so there is a mis-match between expectations and the reality. Guidance and counselling systems have a particular role in encouraging and providing access to the full range of employment opportunities. Evidence from DIECEC cities suggests that this issue needs to be addressed with parents and the 'elders' in communities as well as with the young people themselves.

The education, training and employment opportunities for young ethnic minority women is also a major issue. Many young women who could progress much further within education and training systems are restrained by the cultural norms and traditions within their community. Schools, training, guidance and counselling agencies, further and higher education institutions and employers all have a role to play in working at this issue. Evidence shows that as communities become more established, and as the information about opportunities for young women spreads, so more and more of them are able to progress further. But this is often a long and gradual process, and cities and education and training systems and employers must be aware of the experiences, feelings and traditions of the communities as well as their own desire to see more ethnic minority young women progressing through education and training into employment. In particular, employers need to ensure that their working practices and environment allow these young women to feel and be comfortable and safe.

This theme suggests preparatory, preventative and curative measures which can be put in place to seek to provide appropriate pathways into further education, training and employment for young people from ethnic minority backgrounds, and is illustrated by the following case study.

Theme I: Case Study

Ethnic minority employment and training project in Helsinki

City of Helsinki Education Department: Ulla Kauppinen
Tel: ** 358 9310 86870
Fax: ** 358 9310 86490
E-mail: ulla.kauppinen@edu.hel.fi

The City of Helsinki Education Department has responsibility for the policy, administration and support of vocational education as well as statutory schooling. This allows it to co-ordinate developments between the two sectors and help to ensure coherent progression routes. It also enables the city to maintain an overview of vocational education and training provision and provide to meet supply with demand, as well as catering for the particular needs of specific groups of young people.

The Ethnic Minorities Employment and Training Project is an initiative of the City Education Department. It arose from information from schools and from the City Foreigners Office about the situation of growing numbers of young people from ethnic minorities who, for a variety of reasons often to do with arriving recently in Finland, had not achieved the thresholds which would enable them to progress to training programmes and employment.

The main ethnic minority groups in Helsinki are of Russian, Estonian, Somalian, Vietnamese, Chinese and Bosnian origin. The needs of young people of Somalian origin in terms of education and training are particularly acute.

The Project has three main phases:

* initial evaluation of the trainees education and training experience

* vocational skills testing

* the development of an individual training and employment plan.

A special unit was established in the Division for Vocational and Adult Education and Training of the Helsinki City Education Department. This unit is responsible for the initial evaluation of young ethnic minority people's prior experience of education, training and work experience. The initial evaluation phase lasts for two to three weeks. There are places on this programme for approximately 60-80 people each month.

The vocational skills testing programme aims to evaluate existing vocational skills and assess what further training will be needed. In 1995, assessments were carried out in fourteen different vocational areas. Assessments are carried out by qualified staff in vocational training institutions and the range of institutions involved is expanding. The range of assessments covers:

* language skills in Finnish

* vocational or educational levels and skills

* knowledge of employment possibilities

* where appropriate, suitability for certain vocational pathways and changes of career path, for example where opportunities in Finland differ from those in the country or origin.

The outcomes of these assessments are then developed into an individual training and employment plan which is formulated in discussion with the student. Discussions cover:

* how the assessment outcomes correspond to the student's own objectives and plans

* what the most appropriate next steps should be in terms of meeting the needs identified by the assessment and enabling progression to employment

* what specific steps the student should take to promote and ensure his/her own opportunities and to achieve the objectives of the plan.

The project aims
* to assess the training and education needs and employment prospects of young ethnic minority people

* to carry out rigorous assessments of basic and vocational skill levels so as to develop an individual training and employment plan

- to make the necessary links with education and training provision and with employment opportunities so that the plans can be realised.

The assessments are carried out by trained staff who are experienced at working with and assessing the level of education and training of people from ethnic minorities. Interpreters are used where needed to ensure that areas of competence can be identified even where the young person's knowledge of Finnish does not allow them to explain or demonstrate competence and to draw up the individual training and employment plan.

The training and employment plans are made against the background knowledge of the local and national labour market in Finland and the opportunities available. These sectors of employment may be very different from those for which the young person had received education and training in their country of origin. These factors have to be taken into account in both the assessment and planning phases.

This development is characterised by:

- a thorough and planned process, focusing on the particular situation of ethnic minority young people as individuals

- a positive outcome in terms of the training and employment plan and realistic ways in which it can be implemented

- a process which involves the young people in the decisions about their future training needs and the possibilities of employment for them

- a multi-level approach which involves the co-ordination of organisations such as the City Education Department, the National Labour Office, the City Foreigners Office, Social Services, Vocational Institutions and ethnic minority associations.